LIFE IS SWEET

also by the same author

NAKED
AND OTHER SCREENPLAYS
ABIGAIL'S PARTY and GOOSE-PIMPLES
(Penguin)
SMELLING A RAT and ECSTASY
(Nick Hern Books)

LIFE IS SWEET
Mike Leigh

faber and faber
LONDON · BOSTON

First published in 1994 by
Faber and Faber Limited
3 Queen Square London WC1N 3AU

Photoset by Parker Typesetting Service, Leicester
Printed in England by Clays Ltd, St Ives plc

Introduction © Mike Leigh
Life is Sweet screenplay © Mike Leigh
Life is Sweet photographs © Simon Mein

A CIP record for this book is available from the British Library

ISBN 0–571–17558–9

2 4 6 8 10 9 7 5 3 1

CONTENTS

FOREWORD

In alphabetical order and, amongst other things, *Life is Sweet* is about accordions, affection, alcohol, alienation, anorexia, babywear, ballet, baths, birdcages, birth, boys, bullshit, candles, capitalism, cars, caravans, caring, catering, central heating, chocolate, chips, coffee, cowboy hats, daughters, dieting, disco dancing, do-it-yourself, drums, dying, eatables, energy, enjoyment, Europe, existence, families, fatherhood, fatness, feelings, football, free enterprise, garlic, girls, goldfish, the Goons, guitars, high hopes, holidays, industrial safety, jam, kids, kith, kin, laughter, lies, life, love, lust, Princess Margaret, marriage, money, motherhood, needing, nibbling, nutrition, orthopaedic beds, paranoia, parents, Paris, Piaf, pineapples, plaster dogs, plumbing, politics, prawns, quiche, rape, regrets, restaurants, roast lamb, scarves, second-hand goods, sex, spoons, stuffed dogs, sugar and spice, survival, taking risks, tea, tears, togetherness, tongues, tripe, twins, the USA, violence, warmth, whisky, wine. World War II, X-chromosomes, youth, zeal and zest.

   I wrote this for the film's premiere at the London Film Festival, and, four years later, I would stand by every word . . .

Mike Leigh
London, October 1994

LIFE IS SWEET

Life is Sweet was first shown at the London Film Festival on 11
November 1990.

The cast and crew was as follows:

WENDY	Alison Steadman
ANDY	Jim Broadbent
NATALIE	Claire Skinner
NICOLA	Jane Horrocks
AUBREY	Timothy Spall
PATSY	Stephen Rea
NICOLA'S LOVER	David Thewlis
PAULA	Moya Brady
STEVE	David Neilson
CUSTOMER	Harriet Thorpe
CHEF	Paul Trussel
NIGEL	Jack Thorpe Baker

Written and directed by	Mike Leigh
Produced by	Simon Channing-Williams
Cinematographer	Dick Pope
Editor	Jon Gregory
Production Designer	Alison Chitty
Costume Designer	Lindy Hemming
Music	Rachel Portman
Sound Recordist	Malcolm Hirst

A Thin Man Film
for Film Four International
with the participation of British Screen.

WENDY *is taking a group of about twenty-five little* GIRLS *for a Saturday morning dancing class in a large, sunlit hall. She is dressed in a bright-pink blouse and has a matching bow in her hair.*

The dancing is relaxed and jolly; WENDY *is more concerned with getting the* GIRLS *to express themselves and to enjoy the rhythm than with anything formal or rigorous. They are all reasonably keen and on the whole they carry out her instructions enthusiastically.*

A tape is playing – cheerful, vulgar and sentimental (Portman & Wastall: 'Happy Holidays').

WENDY *is conducting the class from one end of the hall, facing several rows of kids.*

To begin with, we see all this for a few moments through the windows of two pairs of glass-panelled doors.

WENDY: All right, Suzie . . . are you ready? Just move a little bit that way, darlin'. That's it. OK, after four . . . One, two, three, four! Stretch! Yeah! Round . . . stretch!
(*We cut inside the hall.*)
That's a good girl, Lucy! One, two, three, stretch! One, two, three . . . One, two, three, four! Round, smile! One, two, three . . . and one, two, and cha-cha-cha! One, two, and cha-cha-cha! Very good . . . doing well. And again – one,

4

two, three, stretch, one, two, three, four! Get your legs up!
That's better! Stretch, right up! Like you're stretching for
sweets on the top shelf! Cha-cha-cha! One, two, and cha-cha-
cha! Very good . . . come on! One, two . . . Woo!! Come on,
enjoy yourselves!
(WENDY *now leads the* GIRLS *round the hall in an informal
circle.*)
Right, put your hands on your hips, like that. Yeah, that's it.
And the other one! Now wave with both hands! Right?
That's it. Very good – come on, Laura, you can be leader
now. Right out here . . . keep to the edges – that's right!
Let's have a bit of a bum-swing from you! Above your heads
– come on, hands up! Oh, swing those bums! That's it. And
you're doing that cleaning your mum's windows. (*Circular
hand motion.*) All right? And then you see your best friend
. . . so you're shoutin' out, 'Hi! It's me! I'm here!' (*Waving
with both hands.*) Say, 'Hi!'
GIRLS: Hi!
WENDY: Hi!
GIRLS: Hi!
WENDY: Say, 'It's me!'
GIRLS: It's me!
WENDY: 'I'm here!'
GIRLS: I'm here!
WENDY: 'Gimme a five-pound note!'
GIRLS: Give me a five-pound note!
WENDY: 'I wanna go and spend it on sweets!' I thought that'd get
you smilin'! Thought you'd like that! Come on, 'oo's goin'a
be the leader now, then?

A few minutes later. WENDY *walks over to the girls' coats and things,
which are hanging on rows of hooks.*
WENDY: Right – come on, then . . . time to go home! Not too
much of a rush now – I don't want you trippin' over!
(*The* GIRLS *crowd round and collect their belongings.*)
Right, get your coats and shoes on outside, as usual. All
right, d'you wanna put your little cardigan on, Suzie? Eh?
Put it on, 'cos you might get a little chill. Got your sleeves
inside out – get your coats, now! If you can't reach your

5

bags, I'll get them down! 'T's it, put your cardie on – hope
your headache's better soon!
(WENDY *helps* SUZIE *on with her cardigan.*)
GIRL: My bag's next door.
WENDY: All right? 'Bye, darlin' – bye!
GIRL: My bag's next door!
WENDY: Your bag's next door? All right, don't worry. 'Oo's is the
green coat?
(*She holds up the green coat.*)

*Later the same morning – a bright, sunny day outside Wendy's and
Andy's small terraced house.*

ANDY *is leaning in his front doorway, watching the world go by. He
is holding a can of lager.*

A young woman walks past with a child in a push-chair.

*An old Citroën estate swings into the parking space (a concrete patch
where once was a front garden).* ANDY *gestures half-serious
manoeuvring instructions to the driver, then steps forward and opens
her door – it is* WENDY.

*This action is held for a while in long-shot from the other side of the
road and the following dialogue (down to 'it's lethal') can only just be
heard under the film music, the atmosphere being more important than
the substance at this early stage.*

WENDY: Innit hot?
ANDY: Gorgeous!
WENDY: Tell you what, Andy . . . you're lucky I'm not in the
hospital!
ANDY: What?
(*She hands him a carrier bag full of shopping.*)
WENDY: That door, swung back, nearly took me leg off again!
ANDY: It's the hinge, innit?
WENDY: Yeah! It's that catch . . . it's gone. (*She has got out of the
car. She is wearing sun-glasses.*)
ANDY: I'll 'ave a look at it later.
(*They close the car door.*)
WENDY: It's lethal!
(*We cut closer and from now on the dialogue is audible.*)
Oh, I wish you'd do something with this porch! (*An
unfinished wooden structure.*)

6

ANDY: I will do!

WENDY: 'T's embarrassin'! (*She stops in the doorway.*)

ANDY: Just got to get the rest of the timber – that's all!

WENDY: Oh, And' – you've been saying that for two years.

ANDY: Take these boards up to 'ere, bang a bit o' trellis on the outside, slap a coat o' white paint on it, get some nice creepers growin' up it, look lovely!

WENDY: I don't want trellis, Andy – it'll look like a Chinese restaurant!

ANDY: That'll be nice!

> (WENDY *turns to go into the house just as* NICOLA *scurries out of the living room and up the stairs, wearing a nightie.*)

WENDY: Oh, 'allo!

NICOLA: Oh, shut that door, it's freezin'!

ANDY: Oh, you've finished, 'ave you?

NICOLA: No, I'm still in the bath!

ANDY: Wouldn't surprise me!

WENDY: Made a mess, 'ave yer?

NICOLA: No!

WENDY: (*Imitating* NICOLA) 'No!'

> (NICOLA *disappears at the top of the stairs.* WENDY *goes into the room.* ANDY *starts to close the front door.*)

ANDY: Oh, 'allo!

> (NATALIE *is just arriving with her bicycle. She pushes it up the path.*)

NATALIE: All right?

ANDY: Where you been?

NATALIE: Town.

WENDY: 'Allo, Nat!

ANDY: What you been doin'?

NATALIE: Shoppin'.

> (ANDY *closes the front door.* NATALIE *takes her bike round the back of the house through a narrow tunnel.*)

Minutes later, in the kitchen. WENDY *bustles about.* ANDY *swigs his lager.* NATALIE *comes in, puts on the electric kettle and proceeds to make coffee.*

WENDY: D'you wanna little sandwich, Andy?

ANDY: Yeah – what you got?

WENDY: Cheesie-toastie?

ANDY: Yeah, lovely!

WENDY: Still got me glasses on (*Laughs*) . . . thought I was goin' blind! (*She takes them off. Then she produces a large bar of chocolate from the carrier bag.*) Here y'are.

ANDY: D'duh! Chocolate!

WENDY: You're chocaholic, you are!

ANDY: You are! I could give it up tomorrow – no trouble! (*He strolls over to the window.*)

NATALIE: D'you want coffee?

ANDY: No, thanks!

WENDY: Please! D'you wanna little sandwich, Nat?

NATALIE: Yeah!

WENDY: D'you want pickle?

NATALIE: 'Course I want pickle!

(WENDY *gets a jar of pickles out of the fridge.*)

ANDY: Going to get out there this afternoon . . . finish off that patio.

WENDY: Oh, don't give me a heart attack, Andy, please!

ANDY: I will! Make a start. What d'you get, Nat?

NATALIE: A shirt.

ANDY: Is this it?

NATALIE: Yeah.

ANDY: Can I 'ave a look?

NATALIE: If you want to.

(*He gets it out of its bag.* WENDY *is washing her hands.*)

ANDY: Oh, it's nice!

NATALIE: Yeah, it's all right, innit?

ANDY: Yeah.

WENDY: Why d'you always get a man's? (*She dries her hands on a towel.*)

NATALIE: 'Cos I like 'em.

ANDY: Suits me. Thanks a lot, Nat!

NATALIE: Funny man.

ANDY: It's not for me?

NATALIE: No, 's not for you . . .

ANDY: Oh. Shame – thought me luck'd changed.

(WENDY *examines the shirt.*)

WENDY: You should get a nice blouse, short sleeves. Well, show yourself off a bit.

(NATALIE *takes the shirt and folds it up*.)

NATALIE: Shut up!

WENDY: Well . . .

ANDY: Don't listen to 'er!

(NATALIE *has put the shirt back in its bag and has left the room, followed by* ANDY. WENDY *does a little dance routine and puts on her apron*.)

NATALIE *goes upstairs. She passes a door on which a handwritten sign warns, 'Private Keep Out'. As she passes,* NICOLA *comes out of this door, her bedroom, and hovers in the doorway of the adjacent bedroom, Natalie's. She is smoking a cigarette.*

NICOLA: Nat.

NATALIE: What?

NICOLA: D'you get me those fags?

NATALIE: No.

NICOLA: Why not?

NATALIE: I told you, you wanna smoke, you can get your own fags.

NICOLA: Well, could you lend me some money?

NATALIE: 'Ow much?

NICOLA: Tenner . . .

NATALIE: What's it for?

NICOLA: All right, a fiver.

NATALIE: Well, what d'you wannit for?

NICOLA: Mind your own business!

NATALIE: Suit yourself.

NICOLA: You'll be chargin' interest next.

NATALIE: Yeah – it's a good idea.

NICOLA: Capitalist! When d'you get that?

(NATALIE *is putting the new shirt on a hanger*.)

NATALIE: 'S morning. 'S all right, innit? (*She holds it up*.)

NICOLA: No . . . looks like a tea-towel. (*She leaves*.)

NATALIE: Yeah, I was quite pleased with it myself.

NICOLA, *now out of* NATALIE's *sight, gives her a famous obscene sign, goes into her room and slams the door.*

A few minutes later. WENDY, ANDY *and* NATALIE *are sitting around*

in the living room. WENDY *and* NATALIE *have large coffee-mugs.*
ANDY *still has his can of lager.* ANDY *and* NATALIE *are both reading
newspapers.* NICOLA *comes in, sits down and puts on her canvas
lace-up shoes.*

WENDY: 'Ey, Andy – guess what.

ANDY: What?

WENDY: I woke up this morning . . . I felt a little bit whatsit,
    y'know, an' I thought to meself, 'Oh, blimey! Don't tell me
    I'm in the family way!' (*Laughing.*)

ANDY: Jesus Christ!

NICOLA: What's 'the family way' supposed to mean?

NATALIE: You know what it means.

NICOLA: No – I know what 'pregnant' means.

ANDY: You don't 'arf talk some rubbish.

NICOLA: Well, silly little sayings!

WENDY: Oh, shut up!

NICOLA: You shut up!

WENDY: I was lying there, Andy, I thought to meself, 'Ah . . . I'd
    love another little baby!'

NATALIE: You're too old to 'ave a baby, in't you?

WENDY: 'Course not!

ANDY: You may not be – I am. (*Neddy Seagoon voice*) You
    wouldn't see me for dust, I tell you!

WENDY: (*Laughing*) Oh, don't Andy – don't be rotten!

NICOLA: Typical. Typical man!

WENDY: Oh, shut up – what d'you know about men?

NICOLA: Enough.

    (NATALIE *looks carefully at* NICOLA.)

WENDY: Anyway, I thought to meself, 'Ah, never mind . . . I'll
    just 'ave to wait till I'm a grandma!' (*Giggling.*)

NATALIE: You're goin'a 'ave a long wait.

NICOLA: Yeah!

WENDY: Eh?

ANDY: 'Oo'd want them?

NATALIE: Oh, that's nice!

WENDY: Stick a couple of brown papers bags over their 'eads.

ANDY: Might be able to flog 'em off cheap, sight unseen.

    (WENDY *roars with laughter.* ANDY *joins in.*)

NICOLA: Anyway, I'm not goin'a waste my life!

ANDY: No? What're you doing now, then? Contributing a great deal, aren't you, sitting around on your arse all day?

NICOLA: Yeah, well, I'm thinkin' about it!

ANDY: Oh, yeah, thinking about it – that's the easy bit, isn't it? Thinking about it – anyone can do that! It's doing it's difficult.

NICOLA: Bollocks!

WENDY: Nicola!

(NICOLA *looks resentful.* ANDY *glowers at her.*)

Shame, though, innit? They were such lovely little dolly-whatsits . . . sitting there in their matchin' little outfits.

(*On the mantelpiece, two snapshots of the twins as babies.*)

My little Natilie and my little Nicola! And now look at 'em!

NICOLA: Oh, get the sick-buckets!

WENDY: And when you 'ave a bath, Nicola, don't leave the towels on the bathroom floor, stinkin' wet!

NICOLA: 'Ere we go.

WENDY: Well, 'ow many times 'ave I got to tell you? It's just two simple little movements, down an' up (*Demonstrates*)! – And pop it on the towel-rail.

NICOLA: Don't be patronizin'!

WENDY: And I won't tell you again about using *my* cotton-wool balls. (*She gets up and leaves.*)

NICOLA: Oh, don't be so selfish!

NATALIE: What d'you want two baths a day for, anyway?

NICOLA: What, are you takin' their side now?

NATALIE: I'm not takin' anyone's side, I'm just asking you a simple question.

NICOLA: Yeah – well, don't.

(WENDY *comes in from the kitchen with three toasted cheese sandwiches, each on a plate. She gives one to* ANDY *and one to* NATALIE.)

WENDY: 'Ere y'are, And.

ANDY: Oh, cheers.

WENDY: 'Ere y'are, Nat.

NATALIE: Ta.

(NICOLA *has got out her cigarettes.*)

WENDY: Don't light that cigarette, Nicola – we're eating!

NICOLA: Don't eat.

NATALIE: It's lunchtime – that's what you do at lunchtime, eat.

NICOLA: Well, what's lunchtime anyway? It's only a convention.

ANDY: Nicola, if you want to smoke while we're eating, go up to your room, all right?

WENDY: (*Munching*) Anyway, if you smoked less and you ate more, you wouldn't be sitting there, looking like a skeleton!

NICOLA: Well, it's better than lookin' like a beached whale!

WENDY: Oh, thank you!! (*Laughs.*) Anyway, yer dad likes something to grab 'old of of a night.

NICOLA: What, blubber?

WENDY: No . . . me little love-'andles. (*Laughs.*)
We got a set each, ain't we, Andy?
(*She laughs again.* ANDY *doesn't, though he manages the faintest gesture towards a smile.*)

NICOLA: Oh, you're disgustin'!

WENDY: Oh, shut up!

NICOLA: Those sandwiches stink!

ANDY: Listen, Nicola, I've told you, if you don't like it, you know what you can do!

NICOLA: Yeah, well I'm goin'!

ANDY: Good!

WENDY: Well, go on, then!

NICOLA: In a minute!

NATALIE: Can't go, can yer?

ANDY: What's keeping you, Nicola? Eh?

WENDY: She's bored.

NATALIE: See, you wanna be with us. So why don't you just act normal?
(WENDY *looks at* NICOLA. NICOLA *doesn't look at anybody, but takes a nervous drag on her cigarette.*)

Next day. WENDY, ANDY *and* NATALIE *are sitting round the kitchen table, tucking into a hearty lunch.*

WENDY: Andy . . .

ANDY: What?

WENDY: 'Ow about 'avin' a little go at the patio today? Please.

ANDY: Not today, Wen.

WENDY: Why not?

ANDY: Gonna rain, innit?

NATALIE: It don't look like rain to me.

ANDY: I don't want to get all the sand and cement out and 'ave it piss down on me, do I?

WENDY: Well, 'ave a go at the bathroom, then . . . finish off me tilin'.

ANDY: Yeah . . . could do . . .

WENDY: Really?

ANDY: 'Ang on . . . 'ang on . . .

WENDY: What?

ANDY: Ain't got no grout.

WENDY: Oh, typical . . .

NATALIE: Well, I can get you grout.

WENDY: There y'are.

ANDY: Eh?

NATALIE: From work.

ANDY: Today?

NATALIE: Well, no, not today, it's Sunday. Tomorrow.

ANDY: Waterproof grout?

NATALIE: 'Course it's gonna be waterproof grout, it's for a bathroom.

ANDY: Yeah, well, there's grout and there's waterproof grout, ain't there?

NATALIE: Allow me to know!

ANDY: Just make sure what you get is waterproof grout.
NATALIE: Don't panic, I'll get you waterproof grout!
ANDY: Great. I'll do it next weekend.
WENDY: (*Laughing*) Can I have that in writin', please?
ANDY: I have to say, Wen, this lamb is delicious! (*He is carving some more from the joint.*)
WENDY: Oh, is it? Good! And the tiles are in the cupboard under the stairs – right? (*She laughs.*)
ANDY: Nice and pink . . . beautiful, innit?
NATALIE: Yeah, 's nice!
WENDY: Are you eatin' yours, missis?
NICOLA: What's it to you? (*She turns out to be sitting in the adjacent living room, balancing a plate of food on her knees.*)
NATALIE: She cooked it, that's what it is to 'er.
NICOLA: Oh, shut up, Goody Two-Shoes!
NATALIE: What's it like in the first-class dining compartment, then?
NICOLA: Listen, if I choose to eat in my own space, that's my prerogative, right?
WENDY: 'Ey, d'you wanna glass of low-calorie H$_2$O?
ANDY: Just leave 'er alone . . .
   (NICOLA *gets up and leaves the room.*)
WENDY: Oh, there she goes!
NATALIE: 'T's the Year o' the Horse.

ANDY: Eh?

NATALIE: Chinese.

ANDY: Oh, yeah? D'you want some more?

NATALIE: Yeah.

ANDY: D'you want some?

WENDY: Yeah, go on then. Cut me a nice big juicy slice . . . I like mine nice and juicy! (*She laughs.*)

NATALIE: Mother! (*She pops a piece of meat into her mouth.*)

A little later, NICOLA *is in her room, sitting on the bed. She flicks through a copy of* Diet *magazine. She is smoking. She is not happy.*

Meanwhile, ANDY *is pottering about in his crumbling garden shed. He emerges with an old pair of ladders. He sits down to examine them. A bit comes off in his hand. He casts the ladders to one side and sits, doing nothing. He is wearing a cowboy hat.*

WENDY *and* NATALIE *are watching him through the kitchen window.*

WENDY: No, you can't rush 'im.

NATALIE: Yeah, 'e's 'appy goin' at that speed, in' 'e?

WENDY: Yeah . . . dead slow and stop. (*She laughs.*)

Very soon after this, NICOLA *is coming down the stairs. She is wearing a T-shirt bearing the message 'Bollocks to the Poll Tax'. She stops half-way down; through the window over the door she can see* PATSY. *He has obviously had a drink or two. He stops by the front gate, tries to open it, fails, then sidles round it. He approaches the front door, so does* NICOLA, *but as he knocks, she walks past it and goes into the living room. We hold on the door . . .*

NICOLA: It's the door.

NATALIE: Well, answer it!

NICOLA: It's that Patsy bloke.

WENDY: Open the door, Nicola.

NICOLA: No – I don't know 'im.

WENDY: 'Course you know 'im!

NATALIE: Go on – I've got wet 'ands!

NICOLA: So?

WENDY: Tell you what, Nicola . . . you're an awkward cow.

NICOLA: Oh, don't be sexist!

15

(WENDY *opens the front door.*)

WENDY: Oh, 'allo, Patsy!

PATSY: 'Allo, Wendy!

WENDY: All right?

PATSY: Sorry to bother you on a Sunday, like, but, er . . . I was wonderin' if Andy was in?

WENDY: Yeah.

(NICOLA *is watching from the living-room sofa.*)

PATSY: Only I was 'opin' to catch 'im down in the boozer, like, but . . . got a bit 'eld up.

WENDY: Oh, yeah?

PATSY: 'Ad to go down see me old mum.

WENDY: Ah, did you? Yeah, he's down the bottom of the garden.

PATSY: Oh . . .

WENDY: D'you wanna see 'im?

PATSY: Yeah, all right . . .

WENDY: 'Ere – come in, then.

PATSY: Thanks very much. Terrific . . .

PATSY *enters the house.* WENDY *closes the door.* PATSY *walks through the living room towards the kitchen.*

PATSY: (*To* NICOLA) 'Allo, girls!

NICOLA: 'Allo, boys!

(*In the kitchen,* NATALIE *is washing up. On seeing her,* PATSY *is surprised and confused.*)

WENDY: 'Ang on a minute . . .

(PATSY *looks back at* NICOLA, *to double-check that he has indeed seen her. She returns his look.* WENDY *taps harshly on the kitchen window with a wooden spoon;* PATSY *winces at this.*)

WENDY: Patsy's 'ere! 'T's Patsy!

PATSY: Oh, there 'e is. I'll just slip out and see 'im, if that's all right? (*He proceeds out through the back door.*)

WENDY: Yeah, that's all right, Patsy – go on . . . Just watch yourself on that little step.

PATSY: What? (*He stumbles on the little step.*)

WENDY: That's the one, yeah. (*Laughing.*) Oh, don't!

Much amused, she joins NATALIE. *Through the kitchen window, they watch* PATSY *advance down the garden towards* ANDY.

16

PATSY: (*Arms outstretched*) Andrew!!

ANDY: 'Allo, Patsy – 'ow are you?

NATALIE: Christ, he's in a right state!

WENDY: 'E's 'ad about ten pints. 'Ey – good job 'e's been banned from drivin'!

NATALIE: Nice 'air-style.

(PATSY *joins* ANDY.)

WENDY: Ah, I bet 'is wife did those little streaks. She must've got one of them whatsits – one of them 3.99 kits from the chemist.

(NICOLA *joins* NATALIE *and* WENDY.)

NICOLA: What d'you let 'im in for, eh?

WENDY: What was I supposed to do?

NICOLA: Fascist. (*She leaves.*)

WENDY: Tell you what, though, I wouldn't trust 'im.

NATALIE: I wouldn't trust anyone wearing a suit like that.

WENDY: They cost about three 'undred quid, them suits, you know.

NATALIE: What's 'e do, anyway?

WENDY: 'E don't do anything – 'e's unemployed.

ANDY *goes into his shed;* NATALIE *watches as he sits on an old stool and picks up a stringless, neckless guitar.* PATSY *leans in the doorway.*

ANDY: Lay me 'ands on anything in 'ere. You name it – bit of old rope . . . Christmas tree . . . guitar . . .

PATSY: Ah! The old one-armed guitar player, eh?

ANDY: Yeah! I'm gonna fix it up. Put a new neck on it . . . new set o' strings. Basically, it's a good box. (*Sings in American accent.*) 'Mothers, don't let your children grow up to be cowboys . . .!!'

(*He laughs, slightly embarrassed.* PATSY *laughs too, a little unconvincingly. He glances towards the house for a moment.*)

PATSY: Listen, Andy, er, you want to get yourself out of the house for a while?

(ANDY *holds up and animates, glove-puppet style, a small painted plaster dog.*)

ANDY: (*Neddy Seagoon voice*) Hallo, my friend! (*Normal voice.*) I love 'em. She can't stand 'em – won't let 'em through the door. I got two of them. Car boot sale. (*He picks up the other dog, which is identical. He holds them facing each other and does*

17

a comic growl.) Twins! (*He looks momentarily towards the house.*)

PATSY: 'Ere . . . you got twenty minutes, 'ave yer?

ANDY: What for?

PATSY: I got something for yer!

ANDY: Listen, Patsy, whatever it is, I swear to God I can't afford it – I'm broke.

PATSY: Andrew . . . I am inviting you to accompany me to a certain place . . . where I'm gonna show you somethin'.

ANDY: (*Grinning*) Where? What is it?

PATSY: I am not prepared to reveal that at this stage.

ANDY: Why not?

PATSY: It's a surprise.
     (*Pause.*)

ANDY: What is this?

PATSY: Come on – do yourself a favour!

ANDY: Give us a clue!

PATSY: No! Stum is the word. If you don't go, you'll never know! Be there or be square.

ANDY: Nah . . .

PATSY: All right – suit yourself!
     (ANDY *is still grinning – an intrigued, vulnerable grin.*)

Minutes later, at the front of the house. The door opens and out rushes ANDY *still wearing his cowboy hat. He is followed by* WENDY.

ANDY: I'll see you in a minute.

WENDY: 'Ow long're you gonna be?

ANDY: Be right back.

WENDY: Where you goin'?

ANDY: I don't know!
     (*He opens the car door.* PATSY *comes out of the house.*)

WENDY: Where are you takin' 'im, Patsy?

PATSY: Don't worry, Wendy – a little magical mystery tour.

WENDY: 'Ey, Andy – still got your 'at on!

ANDY: Ooh, blimey . . . catch!

WENDY: Sure you two 'aven't got a woman?

ANDY: What, with my luck?

PATSY: What, with a beautiful girl like you? (*Laughs. He has walked round the car. He gets in.*)

WENDY: Heard it all before! See you later! (*She closes the door.*)
ANDY: See you later!
    (*As the car backs out,* NICOLA *comes to the door.*)
NICOLA: (*Shouting*) Dad!
ANDY: What?
NICOLA: Get us twenty Silk Cut!
ANDY: Get your own!
NICOLA: SELFISH PIG!! (*She slams the door.*)

A little later. NATALIE *comes out of the back door with a garden parasol, followed by* WENDY *with some cushions.*
WENDY: Oh, it's nice an' 'ot!
NATALIE: It's a bit bright, innit?
WENDY: 'T's it. (*She unstacks a white plastic chair and places it in a sunny position.*) That's right . . .
    (NATALIE *is assembling the parasol.*)
NATALIE: Come on, get in.
    (WENDY *unstacks another chair.*)
WENDY: What, can't get it in the 'ole? Shut up! (*Laughing.*)
NATALIE: D'you 'ave to?

Meanwhile, at a scrapyard, Andy's *car is creeping surreptitiously between old cars, oil drums and precarious piles of wooden pallets.*
PATSY: Relax, Andy . . . relax!

Whilst back at the house, a clapped-out red open sports car pulls up, belching smoke everywhere. AUBREY *gets out, stepping over the door rather than through it. He wears sun-glasses and a baseball cap. He adjusts his dress, produces a pineapple, which he tosses in the air and catches, and proceeds jauntily towards the front door.*

All this is watched through the lace curtains by NICOLA. AUBREY *knocks on the door.* NICOLA *glances over her shoulder in the direction of the back garden. Then she answers the door.*
AUBREY: Oh . . . hi, Natalie.
NICOLA: It's Nicola.
AUBREY: Oh, yeah – sorry. Brought a pineapple. (*He displays it.*)
NICOLA: What for?
AUBREY: For your mum . . . y'know?

NICOLA: Oh.
>   (*Pause.* NICOLA *glances over her shoulder again.* AUBREY *fidgets with the pineapple.*)
>   D'you want to come in?
AUBREY: Yeah . . . yeah, thanks very much.
>   (*She moves out of the way. He comes in.*
NICOLA: Shut the door.
AUBREY: Oh, yeah . . . (*He shuts it.*) There you go.
>   (*They stand side by side. Pause. Nicola's hands twitch under her T-shirt.* AUBREY *is still fidgeting with the pineapple.*)
>   Nobody in?
NICOLA: No. D'you want to sit down?
AUBREY: Yeah . . . yeah, thanks very much.
>   (*He crosses the room and sits in an armchair.* NICOLA *watches him, patting her face twitchily.* AUBREY *takes off his sun-glasses and puts them in a side pocket, simultaneously producing from an inside pocket a pair of regular spectacles, which he puts on. Then more fidgeting with the pineapple, as he glances round the room.*)

Back at the scrapyard, ANDY *and* PATSY *are inspecting a dilapidated old caravan trailer on which is painted 'Hot Snacks'.* ANDY *roars with laughter.*
PATSY: So . . . Andrew, what do you think?
ANDY: I think it's a load of old crap, that's what I think!
PATSY: What's the matter with it?
ANDY: Look at the state of it!
>   (*They walk round the caravan.*)
PATSY: Ergh – coat o' paint! You're lookin' at the future, mate. This could be . . . the catalyst that sparks the revolution. This is what you've always wanted.
ANDY: I want this like I want a hole in the head.
PATSY: This is your chance to break out of the rat race.
>   (*Another howl of mirth from* ANDY. *Suddenly, the open bonnet of a rusting car snaps shut. The two men clutch each other in shock.*)
>   Ooh!

Whilst WENDY *and* NATALIE *are sitting in the garden, browsing through magazines.*
NATALIE: We should get a cat.

WENDY: Eh?

NATALIE: Get another cat, like Tigger.

WENDY: What, a little kitten?

NATALIE: Yeah.

WENDY: No . . . I don't wanna moggy scratching all me furniture. Why, d'you wanna cat?

NATALIE: No . . . I don't know why I said it, really.

(*An ice-cream van plays its tune nearby.*)

WENDY: Could get a big rottweiler. Then it might eat Nicola.

(*She laughs.*)

NATALIE: 'T's a good idea.

WENDY: That's one way of gettin' rid of 'er.

NATALIE: Should get a crocodile.

(*A slight laugh from* WENDY.)

NICOLA *is sitting near* AUBREY *in the living room. She is pulling at her hair.*

NICOLA: My 'air's fallin' out.

AUBREY: Yeah, well . . . stop pulling it, then.

NICOLA: Still falls out.

AUBREY: 'S really nice hair.

NICOLA: You taking the piss?

AUBREY: No. I mean it. I'm sincere.

NICOLA: Bollocks!

AUBREY: You're a really attractive girl, you know?

NICOLA: No, I'm not. I'm too fat.

AUBREY: Fat! What is fat? 'T's all in the mind.

(*Pause.* AUBREY *plays with the pineapple.*)

NICOLA: D'you wanna put it down?

AUBREY: Yeah. (*He does so.*) . . . I think it's on the turn. I didn't wanna waste it. I had a few ideas, but . . . y'know?

NICOLA: Why didn't you eat it?

AUBREY: Great knees.

(*She pulls her skirt over them and pats her face twitchily.*)

Back at the scrapyard. ANDY *is prodding the caravan.*

ANDY: Look at this . . . rust everywhere.

PATSY: There you go, lightning strikin' a cuppa tea (*Referring to a drawing on the caravan of a hot cuppa*).

21

ANDY: It's falling apart. Strong wind, roof'll come off.

PATSY: 'Ere y'are – 'ave a look inside. (*He throws* ANDY *the key to the door, simultaneously opening the door without unlocking it.*)

ANDY: I'm not going in there, mate – I value my 'ealth too much.

PATSY: No, no, feel free!

(ANDY *inches towards the door.*)

ANDY: No way! Phaw . . . ripe, innit? (*He looks in.*)

PATSY: Oh, it's just a bit musty. Needs a bit of air through it.

ANDY: What's the betting somebody died in 'ere. You sure this is on the level, Patsy?

PATSY: Course it is – belongs to my brother!

ANDY: Ha-ha! Look, the old griddle! (*He climbs into the caravan.*)

PATSY: Ah, there she is – beautiful! (*He leans in the doorway.*)

ANDY: Yeah – haven't seen those in a while.

PATSY: She's still in good nick, though . . .

ANDY: You must be jokin'. It's fucked, innit?

PATSY: It's got everything you need in 'ere. (*He looks over his shoulder.*)

At the same moment, WENDY *opens her living-room door.*

WENDY: I'm makin' a tea, Nicola – d'you want one? Oh, 'allo Aubrey . . .

AUBREY: Hallo, Wendy.

WENDY: What're you doin' 'ere?

(*Pause.*)

AUBREY: I brought you a pineapple. (*He stands up and gives it to her.*)

WENDY: Oh, did you? Oh (*Laughs.*) . . . Oh, innit a big one? (*She 'weighs' it, laughing.*) Andy's not 'ere. 'E's just popped out.

AUBREY: Yeah?

WENDY: 'Ow long you been 'ere?

AUBREY: Oh, fifteen, twenny minutes.

WENDY: Oh, you 'aven't, Aubrey!

AUBREY: Straight up.

WENDY: Nicola!

NICOLA: What?

WENDY: Why didn't you tell me Aubrey was 'ere? You knew I was sittin' out the back.

NICOLA: No, I never!

WENDY: Yes, you did.

NICOLA: Are you calling me a liar?

WENDY: Yes, I am calling you a liar.

NICOLA: I thought you'd gone for a walk.

WENDY: Don't be so stupid – I've never been for a walk in me life, 'ave I? Sorry about this, Aubrey.

AUBREY: No sweat.

WENDY: Come and 'ave a little sit in the garden. Take your coat off – get the sun on yourself.

(*She leads him out.*)

AUBREY: Well, she's a nice girl.

WENDY: Yeah, nice with 'er 'ead in a bucket!

(*She giggles uproariously;* NICOLA *imitates this bitterly to herself.*)

Meanwhile . . . 'Bacon Eggs Sausage Burgers' is printed on the serving-hatch of the caravan, which is now opened from the inside by PATSY. ANDY *is busily sorting out old saucepans and utensils.*

PATSY: Look at that – brilliant! Tell you what, mate, I'll let you 'ave these comestibles for nothing! (*He performs a quick burst of mock electric guitar, using a serving spoon, and puts the price list in position.*) I promise you, Andy . . . you go down White Hart Lane, on a Saturday, for the 'ome games . . . (*He comes out of the caravan and talks to* ANDY *through the hatch.*) A man o' your skills? A couple of 'undred beefburgers, you'll make a fortune, I'm telling you. ''Scuse me, governor! I'll 'ave four 'amburgers, three eggburgers, a sausage roll with onions, a bacon, egg and cheese roll, a tea, a Bovril and a large vodka.' (*More electric guitar.*) Sold to the man with the beard! (ANDY *stops sorting out the equipment.*)

ANDY: I 'ave to admit, Patsy . . . I am tempted . . . (*He looks round the caravan.*)

In the sunny back garden of the house, WENDY, NATALIE *and* AUBREY *sit round the table with its parasol.* NICOLA *hovers by a wall.*

AUBREY: (*Sings*) No . . . no regrets,

No. No regret *rien*!

(*He accompanies himself by drumming on his knees with his hands.*)

WENDY: Oh, yeah, that's right – I remember, yeah.

23

NICOLA: She sang it in French!

AUBREY: Yeah, she was from France.

NICOLA: She was thin.

AUBREY: She was thin, she was French.

WENDY: Dead now, isn't she?

AUBREY: Yeah, she was a prostitute.

NICOLA: So?

NATALIE: Shut up!

AUBREY: The Sparrow.

WENDY: Yeah, the little Sparrow – that's right, yeah. So you all set, then, Aubrey? Got all your little menus printed up, an' everything?

AUBREY: Well, yeah . . .

WENDY: Yeah, good.

AUBREY: No, I 'aven't, actually.

WENDY: Oh, blimey! When d'you open?

AUBREY: Tuesday.

WENDY: Well, that only gives you a couple o' days.

NATALIE: 'Ow's everyone meant to know what they want to eat?

NICOLA: They might not want to eat!

WENDY: Oh, 'ere we go!

NATALIE: Don't be stupid – it's a restaurant.

NICOLA: So?

AUBREY: It's all right by me if they don't want to eat . . .

NICOLA: See!

AUBREY: They can bask in the atmosphere.

WENDY: Oh, blimey – you're not gonna make much profit that way, Aubrey! (*Laughs.*)

AUBREY: No *mangaré*, no sweat.

NATALIE: That's daft!

NICOLA: No, it in't!

AUBREY: Parisian.

WENDY: Why, don't they eat in Paris, then? (*She laughs.*)

AUBREY: Good one!

And in the caravan . . .

PATSY: Seven.

ANDY: Two-fifty . . .

PATSY: I'll come down to six.

ANDY: Make it three 'undred.

PATSY: Five-fifty.

ANDY: I'll give you three 'undred now, and fifty when I've
checked out the gear.

PATSY: Five 'undred.

ANDY: Four 'undred.

PATSY: Four-fifty.

ANDY: Four twenty-five.

PATSY: All right – done!

ANDY: Right!

PATSY: It's a deal.

ANDY: Cheers!

A little later, back outside the house, ANDY *is preparing to unhook the caravan from his car.* PATSY *watches.*

ANDY: Unhooked!

PATSY: 'Ang on, 'ang on, drop the wheel!

ANDY: Drop the wheel . . . lovely . . . And – hup!

PATSY: Yeah!

> (*The towbar drops to the ground.*)

ANDY: Hey! How about that? Sweet as a nut.

PATSY: Genius.

ANDY: Just get parked up, be right back. (*He jumps in his car.*)

PATSY: Off you go!

> (PATSY *looks at his watch, heaves a sigh of relief and leans on the caravan. It moves slightly. The car drives off.*)

A few minutes later. ANDY *is guiding* WENDY *out towards the caravan, blindfolding her from behind, with his hands.*

> *The whole of this scene is shot from inside the caravan, framing the characters through the windows and door.*

ANDY: And –

WENDY: Oh, Andy . . .

ANDY: D-dah!! (*He removes his hands.*)
What d'you think?
> (*She looks at the caravan for a moment, then erupts into what for* WENDY *is rather a mirthless laugh.*)

WENDY: Oh, Andy – you 'aven't!

ANDY: She loves it, Patsy! (*He opens the caravan door.*) Look at it:

26

mobile gold-mine – I can feel it in me water!

(NATALIE *and* NICOLA *appear.* AUBREY *looks into the caravan.*)

WENDY: Oh, Andy – you're jokin' me!

ANDY: I'm not, I promise – God's truth, no word of a lie!

NICOLA/NATALIE: (*Together*) 'Ave you bought it?

ANDY: Yeah. Good innit?

NICOLA: No.

NATALIE: (*Ironical*) Great!

ANDY: What d'you reckon?

NICOLA: Not much.

(WENDY *has joined* PATSY. ANDY *is bobbing eagerly around the caravan.*)

WENDY: Andy! It's a 'eap o' rubbish!

ANDY: What d'you mean?

WENDY: Well, look at it.

ANDY: Got character, en it?

WENDY: (*Laughing*) Oh, Andy!

ANDY: I love it.

NICOLA: It's disgusting! (*She takes a drag on her fag.*)

ANDY: Eh?

NICOLA: It's ecologically unsound.

(ANDY *is looking through the doorway again.*)

ANDY: You're ecologically unsound.

NICOLA: Bollocks!

(*He joins* NATALIE, *putting his arm round her.*)

ANDY: What d'you reckon, Nat?

NATALIE: It's embarrassin'.

ANDY: Eh? No, you and me . . . soon get it licked into shape.

NATALIE: You must be jokin'!

(*She walks away.* ANDY *looks through the window, then goes back for another look through the door, whilst . . .*)

WENDY: It's all rusty.

PATSY: No, no, Wendy, that is just superficial – know what I mean? Bit of treatment, nice coat of paint – come up lovely!

WENDY: This is you, isn't it?

PATSY: Eh?

WENDY: Oh, Patsy!

(AUBREY *is testing the window.*)

PATSY: 'Scuse me, mate . . . if you don't mind!

AUBREY: What? Oh, yeah, yeah . . . cool.
(ANDY *joins them again.*)
ANDY: Innit great, Aub?
AUBREY: Yeah, yeah, yeah, it's er . . . the possibilities are, er . . .
y'know?
ANDY: Yeah, it's all there. The works. All you need.
WENDY: Where're you gonna keep it, Andy? 'Cos you're not
keepin' it here.
ANDY: I'll get a lock-up or something.
PATSY: Andy . . . (*Indicating the time.*)
ANDY: I'll be right with you, mate. Just get me whatsit.
WENDY: Andy! What's goin' on, Patsy?
PATSY: Nothing!
WENDY: Well, 'ow much is 'e payin' you for it, then?
PATSY: Well . . . that is not for me to say, Wendy.
(AUBREY *has another peep through the doorway.*)

In the house, ANDY *grabs his jacket.* NICOLA *is sitting on the sofa, still
smoking.*
NICOLA: You're behaving like a big kid.
ANDY: (*Leaving*) Don't be cheeky! (*He rushes out of the house,
putting on the jacket.*) All right, Patsy?
PATSY: Right.
WENDY: Andy – where're you goin'?
ANDY: Ten minutes, Wen!
WENDY: Where're you goin'?
ANDY: I'll be right back!
PATSY: Bye, Wendy.
WENDY: Andy!
(ANDY *and* PATSY *make off towards the car on the other side of the
road.*)
WENDY: What's 'e doin'?
NATALIE: 'E's gettin' conned.
WENDY: As usual.
(*Suddenly the caravan tips up.* AUBREY *has got inside. There is a
loud crash as pots and pans hurtle about.*)
Aubrey! Are you all right?!
(AUBREY *gets out and the caravan reverts to its horizontal position.*)
Oh, blimey. (*Laughs.*) I thought you'd copped it then.

28

AUBREY: Yeah, it sort of . . . went up on me there, I . . .
WENDY: Yeah! There's no whatsit – whatsit, legs under there, is
there?
(WENDY *takes* AUBREY *into the house, as* NATALIE, *watched by*
NICOLA, *squats down to inspect the caravan.*)
AUBREY: I wondered what was 'appening, it's . . . yeah, I know.
WENDY: Listen, 'ave a cup of tea.

At a cash-dispenser outside a bank, ANDY *draws out some money and
gives it to* PATSY.
PATSY: Ah, jackpot!
ANDY: There you go, mate.
PATSY: Thanks very much, Andy. All right, mate . . . see you
through the week. (*He shakes Andy's hand.*)
ANDY: Don't you wanna lift?
PATSY: No – I've got to go and see me old mum.
ANDY: Oh, all right!
PATSY: Know what I mean? (*He leaves.*)
ANDY: Right, cheers – all the best! (*He leaves in the opposite
direction.*)

Back home in his living room, ANDY *is standing looking out of the
window at his caravan.* WENDY *is sitting beside him in an armchair.*
AUBREY *is squashed on the sofa between* NATALIE *and* NICOLA, *who
holds his cap whilst he smooths his hair, using his reflection in the
coffee table. When he's finished, she gives it him back and they share a
moment together.*
ANDY: To be honest with you, it's worth far more in scrap value
alone than what I paid for it.
WENDY: (*Laughing*) So what did you pay for it, then?
ANDY: What? Well . . . (*Nervous laugh.*) Well, what I done, I
mean I haven't actually – it depends what you mean by –
WENDY: See, 'e's not crackin' on, Aubrey!
ANDY: No, no, no – I know what I'm doing!
WENDY: (*Laughing*) Could've fooled me!
NATALIE: Well, I hope you didn't pay more'n ten quid for it.
ANDY: Well, I paid more than ten quid for it, yeah – but look at
it, it's an investment, innit?
NICOLA: Tory!

(NATALIE *tuts*.)

WENDY: So what d'you think about it, Aubrey?

ANDY: Yeah, mate?

AUBREY: Er . . . it's . . .

WENDY: Now, be honest!

AUBREY: Yeah, it's – gilt-edged, y'know?

ANDY: See? Aubrey knows the game.

AUBREY: Can't go wrong.

(ANDY *has sat on the arm of Wendy's chair*.)

ANDY: Ronald McDonald 'ad to start somewhere, didn't 'e?

WENDY: Oh, blimey – 's old Big Mac sittin' 'ere, look!!

(ANDY *and* WENDY *both laugh*.)

ANDY: So when we going to see your restaurant then, Aub?

WENDY: Yeah . . .

AUBREY: Whenever you like . . .

WENDY: 'Ave a little nose!

ANDY: Yeah . . . before you open . . . if you want any advice.

NICOLA: 'E wants it to be a success, Dad!

ANDY: Shut up.

NATALIE: Yeah!

AUBREY: I'd love you to see my restaurant. Don't get me wrong,
     I'm confident . . .

WENDY: Yeah.

AUBREY: In fact, I'm mega-confident.

WENDY: Oh, are you?

AUBREY: I just haven't had any outside input, y'know.

WENDY: Oh, 'aven't you?

ANDY: We could go now, Wen.

WENDY: Yeah, all right!

NICOLA: 'E might want to stay 'ere!

NATALIE: Well, what's 'e wanna stay 'ere for?

NICOLA: 'Cos.

NATALIE: 'E can do what 'e likes!

AUBREY: We can go now. Yeah! Cool! Wow! Yeah, yeah, yeah,
     yeah – great!

(AUBREY *gets up*. WENDY *laughs*.)

WENDY: Just give us a minute to powder me nose, then.
     (WENDY *gets up, causing the armchair to tip up, depositing*
     ANDY *on the floor*.)

30

ANDY: Hey!

WENDY: Andy, what are you doing?

ANDY: What?

WENDY: We've seen it all before, you know!

ANDY: (*Neddy Seagoon*) 'He's fallen in the water!!'

NATALIE: Prat!

NICOLA: Boring git!

ANDY: Shut up!

WENDY: You're gonna break a leg one of these days, Andy.

AUBREY: You all right, Andy?

ANDY: Yeah, mate – just muckin' about!

> (NATALIE *and* NICOLA *exchange a look of shared disgust and a lack of amusement at Andy's antics.*)

A little later, Andy's and Aubrey's cars arrive at the Regret Rien Restaurant at exactly the same moment, but from opposite directions. WENDY *is Aubrey's passenger. His soft top is still down.*

WENDY: Aubrey! Oh, blimey! I thought we was going to take off then!

> (ANDY *and* AUBREY *get out of their cars.*)

AUBREY: I'll, I'll have to let you out Wendy, em –

WENDY: Oh, I got no 'andle. I can't get out!

AUBREY: Yeah, I know – that's why I have to come round. (*He goes round to open Wendy's door.*)

ANDY: Ah, it's great, Aub (*Referring to restaurant*)!

WENDY: 'Ey, Andy . . . I thought we were going to fly then! (*She laughs.*)

ANDY: Did you? Enjoy the joyride, did you?

AUBREY: So there it is . . .

> (WENDY *is emerging from Aubrey's car.*)

WENDY: I can't get out . . .

ANDY: Oh, it's fantastic, innit, look? Look, Wen . . .

WENDY: Oh, innit posh?

ANDY: (*Reads*) '*Très* exclusive.'

> (WENDY *joins* ANDY *in front of the restaurant as* AUBREY *unlocks the door.*)

WENDY: Is it nice, Andy?

ANDY: Yeah, great.

WENDY: Yeah!

ANDY: It's in good nick, innit?

WENDY: Yeah! – I like the lamps.

ANDY: Yeah!

(*They all gather round the door.*)

WENDY: Oh, that's where you're gonna keep your little menus is it, in there?

AUBREY: Yeah – I can't find the key, though.

ANDY: Well, you need a key, Aub!

(WENDY *and* ANDY *laugh.*)

Moments later, inside the restaurant, a stuffed cat's head returns our gaze. WENDY *screams.*

ANDY: What?

WENDY: Oh, what is it?

(ANDY *laughs.*)

WENDY: Oh . . . it's a little pet cat, look . . .

(AUBREY *picks the head up and animates it.*)

ANDY: (*Neddy Seagoon*) 'It's a dead moggy!'

WENDY: Ah, bless 'im!

(ANDY *and* WENDY *are both laughing.*)

AUBREY: Yeah, it's fantastic, innit? (*He walks over to a small framed photograph of Edith Piaf on the wall.*) I was gonna put this up 'ere. (*He removes Piaf's portrait and replaces it with the cat's head.*)

WENDY: Oh, you can't!

ANDY: No, not in a restaurant, Aubrey. Put people off their food.

WENDY: No, it'll smell!

ANDY: Yeah.

(*Below the cat hangs a Second World War gas mask.*)

AUBREY: See, what I'm going for here is, um . . . the street . . . er, the war . . .

ANDY: Yeah?

(AUBREY *picks up two incomplete accordions.*)

AUBREY: And I've got these accordions from a car boot sale, and I'm gonna stick 'em up 'ere and, er . . . they are going to represent the, er, music of Paree. (*He positions them around the cat and the gas mask.*)

ANDY: Do they work, Aubrey?

AUBREY: No, they're knackered. (*He throws one of them away.*) I got the three of them for seventeen pound fifty – y'know?

ANDY: They saw you coming, mate!

(ANDY *and* WENDY *guffaw loudly.* AUBREY *looks at them, neither offended nor amused. Then he walks away.*)

AUBREY: Yeah, and the birdcages – I'm gonna 'ang them up all over the ceiling.

ANDY: Oh, yeah, you've got a load of them, in't you?

(AUBREY *picks up one of the many birdcages and climbs on to two chairs. These he walks a few paces, rather as though they were a pair of wooden clogs.*)

AUBREY: They are going to, er . . . symbolize . . . the Sparrow.

(*He hangs the cage on a hook in the ceiling.*)

ANDY: Ah, I like the bike!

(ANDY *walks over to the bicycle parked in the window and decorated with a string of onions and an old beret.*)

WENDY: Oh yeah – oh, innit novel?

AUBREY: Yeah – 's brilliant, isn't it?

ANDY: The old onion-seller!

(AUBREY *gets off the chairs and picks up a rubber plant.*)

AUBREY: That's in the wrong place!

(*He throws it, slightly violently, into a corner, where it lands with a crash.*)

WENDY: Oh, blimey! (*She giggles.*)

ANDY: Is this the original French article, Aubrey?

AUBREY: Yeah, yeah.

(ANDY *puts on the beret for a moment and does a mock-French voice.*)

No, it was me dad's, actually – yeah, it was in the shed.

WENDY: Ah . . . in't that nice, Andy? Ah, 'e would've been proud of you, Aubrey!

AUBREY: No, I don't think 'e would've cared less, Wendy – y'know? . . . He was a nasty old bastard. (*He strides between the tables, picking up another birdcage as he passes it, and putting it down violently enough for bits of it to drop off.*) 'Ere, look at this . . . (*He switches on an illuminated aquarium.*)

WENDY: Oh, you got a fish tank?

ANDY: That's good, innit?

(ANDY *and* WENDY *join* AUBREY.)

WENDY: Oh, yeah!

(ANDY *laughs*.)

ANDY: I thought they were real!

(*They are plastic.* WENDY *roars with laughter.*)

WENDY: So did I! Ah, the fish look a bit 'umpty, don't they?

ANDY: Water's murky, innit?

AUBREY: Yeah, I'm gonna put a couple of lobsters in there. And people can choose 'em . . . and I'm gonna cook 'em, *à la minute*, y'know?

ANDY: Nice one!

Minutes later, in the cluttered restaurant kitchen, AUBREY *is showing them one of his specialities: a white circle on a red sauce on a black plate.*

WENDY: Yeah, so . . . where you gonna put your prawns, then?

AUBREY: Prawn.

WENDY: Is that all – just one? (*She giggles.*)

AUBREY: King Prawn.

WENDY: Oh, sorry!

AUBREY: Anywhere you like, Wendy, y'know? (*He opens the fridge and takes out a prawn.*) It's all a matter of what picture you wanna paint.

WENDY: You 'avin' all black plates, then?

AUBREY: Yeah – great canvas.

ANDY: What's the sauce you're using there, Aub?

(AUBREY *places the prawn in the centre of the plate.*)

AUBREY: Basically . . . jam, blended with orange juice.

ANDY: Orange juice . . .

WENDY: What's that white stuff – cream?

ANDY: No, it's fromage frais, innit?

AUBREY: Yoghurt.

ANDY: Is it?

AUBREY: I think you'll find that fromage frais will bubble on you, And.

ANDY: It needn't. (*He has a look round the kitchen.*)

AUBREY: I achieve this effect by, er . . . gently . . . easing . . . teasing . . . and squeezing. (*He demonstrates this with a piping bag.*)

WENDY: Oh, don't be so dirty!

AUBREY: . . . until you've got a nice symmetrical circle. (*He picks*

34

up a large knife.) And, er . . . then we, er, chisel in the pattern with the end of a knife, and Bob's yer uncle, it's ready to set, y'know?

WENDY: Ah, looks nice, though, Andy!

ANDY: Your grill's in a bit of a state, Aubrey!

AUBREY: Is it? Oh, yeah, the, er, the girl can deal with all that.

WENDY: When they startin', then, your girls?

AUBREY: The dogsbody tomorrow and the waitress on Tuesday.

WENDY: Oh, right?

AUBREY: Great team.

A little later, back in the dining room. ANDY *and* WENDY *are on bar stools, watching* AUBREY *behind the bar, lighting seven candles in wine bottles.* ANDY *has a can of lager.*

WENDY: Oh, I love your little candles!

ANDY: Bistro effect, innit?

AUBREY: Yeah – they're great, in't they? I've been trying to get them all the same length. But, er . . . I keep forgetting to blow 'em out, you know? And, er . . . I 'ave to start all over again. I've been through twelve boxes this week.
(*The phone rings.*)

WENDY: Ah, that'll be your first little booking!

ANDY: 'Ere we go!!
(ANDY *and* WENDY *laugh enthusiastically.* AUBREY *answers the phone.*)

AUBREY: 'Allo, the Regret Rien. Oh, hi, Hilary! (*Mouths.*) Hilary. How are you? You in the starting blocks, raring to go? Great! You what? Hang on a minute. (*Untangling receiver cord.*) Say that again . . . (*He takes the receiver into his kitchen, out of earshot.*)

ANDY: Look at the state of this place.

WENDY: Ah . . . shame, innit?

ANDY: I don't think it'll be ready, you know?

WENDY: You want to see the ladies' toilet.

ANDY: Still, all credit to 'im.

WENDY: Ah, bless 'im, yeah!

ANDY: Puts the old caravan in perspective, dunnit?

WENDY: Oh, Andy, please – don't remind me!

ANDY: What d'you mean?

35

WENDY: Well, I don't want it sitting there, do I, for two years, blockin' me view?

ANDY: No, this has inspired me. I want to get back, get down to work, get stuck in.

(*Wendy laughs, ironically.*)

WENDY: Pigs might fly!

(AUBREY *bursts out of the kitchen.*)

AUBREY: Fuck you!! (*He hangs up the receiver, a touch violently. A bit falls off the phone.*)

ANDY: What's up, mate?

AUBREY: Nothing!

(*He picks up a bottle opener and hurls it into the sink. He is very fraught.* ANDY *and* WENDY *are startled.*)

D'you want a cigar, Andy?

ANDY: No thanks, mate – I don't use 'em.

AUBREY: Wendy, would you like a liqueur?

WENDY: No, ta, no, I'm fine.

ANDY: Who was that, then?

AUBREY: My waitress.

WENDY: What, the big girl?

AUBREY: Yeah.

WENDY: The Aussie?

AUBREY: Yeah . . . no, Kiwi. (*With his bare hand, he snuffs out all seven candles, one for each 'fuck'.*) Fuck, Fuck, Fuck, Fuck, Fuck, Fuck, Fuck! Gotta laugh, an't you?

ANDY: What's the matter, then?

AUBREY: She's, er . . . let me down . . . you know?

WENDY: 'Ow d'you mean!

AUBREY: She's going away . . . with 'er boyfriend.

ANDY: When?

AUBREY: Today – she was phoning from 'Eathrow.

ANDY: Where's she going?

AUBREY: Flippin' Prague!

ANDY/WENDY: (*Together*) Aah . . .

WENDY: Oh, that's not right.

ANDY: No, that's not on, mate.

WENDY: No, sorry.

AUBREY: 'T's great, innit? You give someone a break, a chance to better themselves, an opportunity to enter into a brave new

36

venture . . . and what do they do? Piss off to Poland!

WENDY: Well, that's typical Aussie, innit? Travellers.

ANDY: Students.

WENDY: It's Czechoslovakia, innit, Prague?

ANDY: Yeah – is it?

WENDY: Yeah.

AUBREY: It's all right, I can cope . . . I could do it on me own.

WENDY: No, you can't!

AUBREY: Yes, I can! I've come this far so far solo – I can go the whole hog! I can wait on table – I can do that . . . I'm not proud. They can eat in the fucking kitchen!!

ANDY: Aubrey, Aubrey, calm down, calm down. What you've gotta do, you got to get on to an agency, get a waitress over here to cover you till you get yourself sorted out.

WENDY: Yeah. 'Cos you need that little support.

ANDY: That's right.

AUBREY: 'T's all right, Andy . . . Wendy . . . everything's hunky-dory – cool. I'm in complete control. If ever I see 'er again . . . I'll stick a knife in her guts. I'll slice her face off . . . y'know?

(WENDY *and* ANDY *exchange nervous glances.*)

Later, upstairs in Aubrey's flat over the restaurant, he is fervently playing his drum kit. WENDY *appears with her fingers in her ears, and* ANDY *comes in from another room, still with a lager.*

ANDY: Aub, Aub, Aub, Aub, Aub! Jesus Christ, don't the neighbours complain?

WENDY: Me eardrums, please!

ANDY: Oh, dear!

(AUBREY *stops playing and gets up.*)

AUBREY: Sorry! Sorry – I got overexcited. I am so grateful. Thank you. Really, really, from the deepest part of my heart – thank you!

WENDY: Aubrey, shut up – right?

AUBREY: No, no, I'm sincere.

WENDY: Now, listen. You're in trouble, right? And I'm helping you out, 'cos that's what friends are for – that's right, isn't it, Andy?

AUBREY: It's amazing!

37

ANDY: But you 'aven't even done barwork, Wen – let's be honest.

WENDY: No, but I'm confident, I can 'ave a go!

ANDY: Let's face it, 'ave you ever been a waitress?

WENDY: No.

ANDY: No.

WENDY: But I've been waiting on you all these years, 'aven' I? So . . . (*Laughs.*)

ANDY: Yeah, yeah, yeah!

AUBREY: To be totally honest, Andy, I think Wendy'll be a natural, you know? She's got such grace and charm.

WENDY: Thank you, Aubrey!

ANDY: Excuse me, are we talking about the same girl?

(ANDY *and* WENDY *laugh.*)

WENDY: Don't be rotten! Hey, listen – what've I gotta wear?

ANDY: Black – waitress uniform.

WENDY: What, little French maid's outfit? Woo! (*She laughs.* AUBREY *strikes a cymbal.*) 'Ey, Andy – look at 'is face!

AUBREY: No, er . . . anything you like, Wendy – you know? *Comme çi, comme ça* . . . come casual!

WENDY: What? Skirt and blouse type of thing – yeah?

AUBREY: Yeah, great.

(ANDY *has wandered into another room and is flicking through a copy of* Penthouse.)

ANDY: See if you've got anything in pink, Wen.

WENDY: Oh, shut up, you! Listen . . . aren't you gonna pay me?

AUBREY: Oh, yeah!

ANDY: How much?

AUBREY: Twenty-five pound a week.

ANDY: What?

(WENDY *and* ANDY *roar with laughter. They are all now standing in Aubrey's bedroom doorway.*)

WENDY: You're jokin' me!

ANDY: Leave it out! What time's that flight to Prague?

WENDY: Yeah – we'll be on it!

AUBREY: No, no, no, n- n- no – you don't understand . . . that's just the basic . . . for the paperwork, the taxman, y'know?

WENDY: 'Ow d'you mean?

AUBREY: Well, you get to keep all your tips – that's 12½ per cent . . .

WENDY: Yeah?

AUBREY: If you don't get at least a hundred pounds a week, I'll make up the difference.

ANDY: Oh, that's not bad.

WENDY: Oh, that sounds all right, yeah – that'll go towards the 'oliday.

ANDY: Yeah.

AUBREY: I don't wanna talk about money, anyway. You can 'ave what you like – thousand pounds a week, you know?

WENDY: Yeah, all right, you're on! (*She laughs.*)

AUBREY: No, you know what I mean.

ANDY: Is this your passion pit, then, Aub?

WENDY: Oh, yeah – this is where 'e brings all the girls, Andy!

AUBREY: This is the only room I've had decorated.

WENDY: Oh, yeah? It's nice, though, innit? This is what I call a proper boy's room, you know?

ANDY: Yeah.

(*AUBREY has sat on his large bed and is bouncing up and down.*)

AUBREY: Great bed. Orthopaedic . . . three 'undred pounds . . .

ANDY: 'Ow many does it 'old?

(*WENDY and ANDY roar with laughter. AUBREY does a back-somersault on the bed, hits a venetian blind with his feet and crashes to the floor.*)

ANDY: Oh, careful, Aub! Oh, dear me!

WENDY: Aubrey!

ANDY: You all right, mate?

WENDY: What're you doin'? Comin' up for air?

(*AUBREY has discovered a Mickey Mouse baseball cap on the floor.*)

AUBREY: Thought I'd lost that.

(*He puts it on. ANDY shows WENDY a sexy magazine. She silently mouths, 'Oh, don't!' ANDY puts it back on its shelf.*)

WENDY: What, are you lookin' for fivers down there?

(*ANDY and WENDY laugh.*)

Early that evening, outside the house. WENDY *is leaning in the doorway of the caravan.* ANDY *is sitting inside. The serving hatch is open.*

WENDY: No, all I'm saying, Andy . . . is I think you've made a big mistake, that's all.

ANDY: Little beauty, in't she? (*He throws away a piece of old rope.*)
WENDY: I mean, if you'd got yourself a bank loan . . . and bought
   a really decent van, that's one thing, but, I mean, buying
   this, I mean, you're throwing good money after bad.
   (*He has picked up another piece of rope.*)
ANDY: 'Ave we got any bin-bags?
WENDY: I mean, look at all this – it's rubbish!
ANDY: What d'you think I want the bin-bags for – of course, it's
   rubbish! It's all rubbish – I know that! That's why I wanna
   get this lot cleared out – then I can see what I got. (*He stacks
   some old saucepans and a rag.*)
WENDY: Well, I'm sorry, Andy, I can't get any enthusiasm for it.
   (*He picks up a length of wood.*)
ANDY: I know you can't – it's obvious. To be honest with you, I'd
   appreciate it if you could. I could do with a bit of moral
   support.
WENDY: You'll 'ave to get a licence, you know?
ANDY: What?
WENDY: And I'll tell you what, if you park this on someone else's
   pitch, you're gonna get yourself duffed over.
ANDY: I can look after meself.
WENDY: Oh, can yer? 'Ave you ever seen those 'ot-dog fellas?

They're all like that. (*She squashes her nose with her finger.*)

ANDY: (*Laughing*) Don't know what you're talking about!

(NATALIE *has come out of the house and has joined them.*)

WENDY: Lipstick's a bit bright, Nat!

NATALIE: Oh, very amusing!

(WENDY *laughs.*)

WENDY: Where're you going?

NATALIE: Drink.

(ANDY '*aims*' *the bit of wood, gun-like, at* NATALIE.)

ANDY: 'Ave one for me!

NATALIE: Stayin' in?

ANDY: Yeah.

WENDY: Yeah, 'e's got to save up now . . . pay for this 'eap o' whatsit.

NATALIE: Well, so long as 'e's 'appy.

ANDY: That's right, Nat! Thanks a lot – much appreciated!

NATALIE: 'S all right.

WENDY: Goin' in, I'm freezin'. Tell you what, Andy, I 'ope it don't rain tonight. You'll need your snorkel in 'ere in the morning.

(*She goes into the house, laughing.*)

ANDY: I think she likes it – don't you?

NATALIE: Yeah – she's over the moon. See ya. (*She goes.*)

ANDY: See ya. Have a good time!

(*Through the caravan window, he watches her walk away, down the empty street.*)

A bit later. NATALIE *is in a small pub, playing pool with some young friends of both sexes. She takes a shot. A guy encourages her to have another. She does so, then sits down. Another girl takes a shot, an apparently successful one, and she does a little bow . . .*

NATALIE: Oh, very flash! (*She raises her pint of lager and has a swig.*)

That night. WENDY *and* ANDY *are in bed with the light on.* ANDY *is reading a paperback* (*Peter Wright:* Spycatcher).

WENDY: Two 'undred pounds? Oh, Andy! Well, you're not payin' 'im any more, right?

(ANDY *puts down the book.*)

ANDY: Look . . . d'you want me to carry on doing my brain in at that bloody place for the rest of my life?

WENDY: No, of course I don't.

ANDY: Right! So I'll give it a go at weekends, and if it works out, I'll jack in the day job.

WENDY: Andy, you can't jack in your day job without you got something definite to go to, right?

ANDY: On a Bank Holiday weekend, I could make . . . What? Two, two and a half thousand quid?

WENDY: Oh, Andy! You're just a big softy, you are!

ANDY: Well, who's to say? All right, it's a risk – I admit that, but it's a risk worth taking, innit?

WENDY: I suppose if the worse came to the worst, we could always go on our 'olidays in it! (*She laughs a bit.*)

ANDY: That's right – reconvert it to an ordinary caravan.

WENDY: Stick a coupla bunk beds in it . . . 'ave a little bunk-up. (*They are both amused.*)

ANDY: Ooh, yes, please!
(*They cuddle up.*)

WENDY: 'Ey! 'Ey, 'ow about . . . 'ow about . . . (*Aubrey's voice*) 'Orthopaedic, five 'undred quid, you know?' Bouncing up and down on 'is bed!

(*They both laugh and imitate* AUBREY.)

ANDY: 'Orthopaedic – you know?'

WENDY: 'Orthopaedic – you know?' Ah . . .

ANDY: I tell you, you wanna watch out for Aubrey in that
kitchen. 'E'll come up behind you with a cucumber.
(*They both continue to laugh.*)

WENDY: Listen . . . I don't think it'll be a cucumber he'll be
coming up be'ind me with!

ANDY: No, but maybe you fancy him, I don't know.

WENDY: Oh, you're jokin' . . . I'm not that desperate. Ah, bless
'im. I feel sorry for 'im, actually.

ANDY: Yeah, 'e's not a bad bloke, Aubrey.

WENDY: What're you doin'?

ANDY: What?

WENDY: Mm . . . I like it – do it again!

ANDY: I'm not doing anything!
(*She laughs.*)
I'm not!

WENDY: Go on, then . . .
(*He turns off the light. Darkness.*)
Has Nicola come to bed yet?

ANDY: Yeah, I think so.

WENDY: Oh; I tell you what, Andy . . . she gets me in a right
state, that girl. I 'eard meself shoutin' at 'er this mornin', and
I thought, 'This isn't me . . .' I don't recognize meself, you
know, it's 'orrible.

ANDY: Good job they're not identical.

WENDY: Oh, blimey, yeah. (*She laughs.*) Oh, I used to think . . .
oh, it'd be so nice to go to discos together and . . . bring their
boyfriends 'ome. Oh, well – there you go!
(*Pause.*)

ANDY: Buttered muffins!

WENDY: What?
(*Pause.*)

WENDY: Mm . . .

At the same moment, in her room, NICOLA *is kneeling on the floor,
listening to her Walkman. She pulls out a small suitcase from under
the bed and a key from a drawer behind her. She unlocks a padlock*

43

and removes a chain from round the case, which she now opens. It is packed full of assorted confectionery.

Meanwhile, NATALIE *is in her room, sitting up in bed, reading a USA travel brochure.*

Minutes later, NICOLA *is feverishly gorging two chocolate bars and some crisps, and trying unsuccessfully to vomit into a plastic carrier bag.*

Shortly afterwards, she does throw up into the bag, profusely, using a toothbrush to induce herself.

And NATALIE *lies in bed, in darkness, listening to all this through the wall.*

We end this sequence with a long shot of the back of the house. The only light comes from Nicola's window.

Next day, ANDY *is at work. He runs a large industrial kitchen. Wearing his chef's hat and whites, he closes the heavy door of a refrigeration room and embarks on a tour of inspection. He grabs a bit of food from a tray and nibbles it as he goes. A kitchen* PORTER *staggers past him, bearing a large tray of prepared food.*

ANDY: All right, my friend? (*He continues his tour.*) Don't run!!
> (*He rounds a corner of the kitchen and for a moment leans into a large vat of Bolognese sauce.*) More colour.
> (*He passes three* UNDERCHEFS, *who are chopping vegetables.*) Chop-chop!
> (*He circles round a tall* CHEF *with a ponytail, busy slicing carrots.*)
> Are you happy in your work, chef?

CHEF: Over the moon, mate!

ANDY: Someone's got to do it. In this case it 'appens to be you!
> (ANDY *laughs drily and continues his journey. He moves a mobile stainless-steel utensil rack out of his way, passes an* UNDERCHEF *stirring some soup and retires into his tiny office. Closing the door, he sits down, picks up a copy of* Exchange & Mart, *and proceeds to read it.*)

At the same moment, at a kiddies'-wear shop called Bunnikins, WENDY *is serving an infant male customer who is sitting in his push-chair. His middle-class* MOTHER *stands beside him.*

WENDY: Yeah . . . 'cos you are a little chunker! You're a little

44

chunker – you've got two little chunky cheeks, and you've got two little chunky legs, and you're lovely! Yeah! And you're gonna grow up to be a boxer – yeah, a big boxer, or a wrestler. And I bet you're just like your dad, eh? Are you just like your daddy?

CUSTOMER: D'you have anything in navy?

BABY: Da-da.

WENDY: Navy, yeah. Oh, listen, take no notice of me. I get carried away you know, 'cos mine are grown up now.

CUSTOMER: I don't want any pastels.

BABY: Da-da!

WENDY: No, that's right – yeah. 'Cos you . . . are goin' to a weddin', yeah, a little bird told me. Yeah! So let's 'ave a look what we've got. (*She turns to a clothes-rack.*) Now . . . there's that little outfit – that's French, but that's a little but girly, innit?

CUSTOMER: He needs something more sophisticated.

WENDY: More sophisticated, yeah – 'cos 'e's not a girly boy, is 'e? D'you know what I mean? 'E's more a boy's boy – I mean, you couldn't mistake 'im for a girl, could yer?

CUSTOMER: No, he's a boy.

WENDY: Yeah . . . what's 'is name?

CUSTOMER: Nigel.

WENDY: Oh, bless 'im! Little nidgey Nigel! Well, let's see what we got for you, then, Nigel . . . let's 'ave a little look . . . that's a bit baby-baby . . . oh, wait a minute . . . that's nice . . . we sell a lot o' them.

(*She displays a navy and white suit.*)

CUSTOMER: Oh – I don't think so.

WENDY: Oh, it looks nice on – it really does, little sailor's outfit.

And in another part of town, NATALIE *is carrying a new central heating radiator up the stairs of an old house in the midst of renovation. As she fits it into place on the landing, another* PLUMBER *walks into an adjoining room, where he also proceeds to fit a radiator.*

PLUMBER: 'Ow's that old boyfriend, then, Nat?

NATALIE: What old boyfriend's that, then, Steve?

PLUMBER: Come on!

NATALIE: I'm single and carefree, thanks!
PLUMBER: yeah . . . wish I was.

(*They continue to tighten bolts.*)

Meanwhile, an old blue Ford Escort pulls up alongside ANDY's *caravan. A lanky youth in shades gets out. He is chewing gum. He locks his door, and saunters over to the caravan. He takes off his shades, and looks through the window in the door. Discovering that the door is unlocked, he opens it, and looks inside. Then he rings the doorbell of the house, and resumes his inspection of the caravan.* NICOLA *comes to the front door.*
NICOLA: You never said you was coming today!
LOVER: I'm sorry. I'll go, shall I?
NICOLA: No.
LOVER: What's all this?
NICOLA: What's it look like?
LOVER: Fuckin' dump. Like the rest of your 'ouse.
NICOLA: Middle-class wanker!
LOVER: This your old man's? (*He closes the caravan door.*)
NICOLA: Yeah.
LOVER: What, you goin' on 'oliday?

46

NICOLA: Nah – it's what he wants to be buried in!
  (*He emits a mock laugh.*)
  Well, come on!
  (*As he approaches,* NICOLA *closes the living-room door and stands in front of it.*)
LOVER: Oh, that's all right – I didn't want a coffee, anyway!
NICOLA: Well, it's a dump, innit?
LOVER: Yeah.
NICOLA: Well, what're you waitin' for? Go on!
  (*He sets off upstairs. She slams the front door.*)

Minutes, later, in Nicola's room. Her LOVER *sits on the bed. She stands, facing him.*
LOVER: So, what you been doin'?
NICOLA: Workin'.
LOVER: Leave it out!
NICOLA: I 'ave!
LOVER: What sort o' work?
NICOLA: Writin'.
LOVER: Writin'?
NICOLA: Yeah.
LOVER: Writin' what?
NICOLA: A novel.
  (*He laughs.*)
  What's so funny?
LOVER: You writing a novel? What's it about?
NICOLA: Dunno . . . 'aven't started it yet.
LOVER: Am I in it?
NICOLA: No!
LOVER: Is it autobiographical?
NICOLA: 'Course it is.
  (*He puts his foot between her legs.*)
  What're you doin'?
  (*He moves his foot around.*)
  Get off!
LOVER: No . . .
  (*He pulls her down on to him. They kiss for a short while. Then she gets up.*)
NICOLA: 'Old on a minute . . .

47

(She draws the curtains and goes into Wendy's bedroom, where she takes two silk scarves out of a drawer. She returns to her room and closes the door. She stops for a moment, giving him a loving look whilst fidgeting nervously with the scarves. Then she moves to the bed and stands facing him.)

LOVER: Jesus, no.

NICOLA: What?!

LOVER: Not again – it's borin'!

NICOLA: Well, I'm not doin' it, then!

LOVER: Well, don't do it!

NICOLA: Oh, come on!!

> *(Pause. Then, from amongst assorted junk under the bed, she produces a jar of chocolate spread, which she gives him.)*

Here you go . . .

LOVER: No, thanks, I've just eaten.

NICOLA: Ha, ha, wise guy!

> *(She throws the scarves over his head. He removes them.)*

LOVER: Lie down, then. You pervert.

> *(He leans forward and starts preparing one of the scarves, whilst she slips behind him, puts her arms round him, and starts kissing and licking his neck.)*

Shortly later. They are naked, although NICOLA *is still wearing her spectacles. Her wrists are tied to the bed with the scarves. Her breasts are covered with chocolate spread, which her* LOVER *is licking off.* NICOLA *is breathing heavily. He pauses for a moment.*

NICOLA: Don't stop!!

LOVER: I've 'ad enough.

NICOLA: What?

LOVER: *(Laughing)* I can't eat no more – I'm full up!

NICOLA: It's not a joke!

LOVER: I'm gonna puke . . .

NICOLA: You're weak.

> *(He looks at her, then kisses her strongly on the mouth. She responds. They continue to kiss and writhe, as he massages her chocolate-covered breast.)*

Afterwards, in the bathroom. NICOLA *is wearing a dressing gown and is running a bath, into which she pours some bath salts. Her* LOVER *stands in the doorway, dressed. He lights a cigarette.*

NICOLA: Are you going, then?

LOVER: No.

NICOLA: Well, you're not stayin'.

LOVER: Thought I could get in there with yer.

NICOLA: No, you won't!

LOVER: What's the matter with you?

NICOLA: Nothing!

LOVER: I don't agree. (*Shouting.*) Eh?

NICOLA: Don't shout! Sexist pig!

LOVER: Why is shoutin' sexist?

NICOLA: 'Cos that's what men do!

LOVER: You're full o' shit! (*Pause.*) Why is it you never want me
to stay?
(*Pause. She ruffles her hair. He walks out of the house. She
slams the bathroom door.*)

Later, in the kitchen. The washing machine is running. WENDY
walks up to it. She has a duster in her hand.

WENDY: What's in this machine, Nicola?

NICOLA: My bedding.

WENDY: Not again! Why didn't you peg me washin' out?

NICOLA: I'll do it later!
(WENDY *arrives at her display cabinet in the living room, puts
on its special light and starts dusting.*)

WENDY: Blimey, it could've been dry by now! So what you been
doin' all mornin'? Sweet Fanny Adams, as usual. Anybody
ring?
(NICOLA *is leaning against the end of the door.*)

NICOLA: Like 'oo?

WENDY: Like your grandad, for instance.

NICOLA: No!

WENDY: (*Imitating* NICOLA) No! (*Laughing.*) Look at Andy on
this picture!
(*She is dusting a framed photograph of a young* ANDY *amongst
a large group of chefs. They all wear chef's gear.*)
I still reckon 'e looks like Tommy Cooper! (*She laughs.*)
What d'you 'ave for your breakfast?
(*Now she is polishing a ceramic ballet dancer's foot.*)

NICOLA: Big fry-up.

WENDY: No, really.

NICOLA: Toast!

WENDY: I don't believe you, Nicola!

> (*And now she is polishing a framed photograph of a group of little girls, posing in their ballet frocks.* Circa *1959.*)

NICOLA: Can you lend us a couple of quid?

WENDY: What for? (*She squirts some polish from an aerosol can.*)

NICOLA: Packet of fags.

WENDY: No chance!

NICOLA: Mean cow!

> (WENDY *is polishing some small ballet trophies – a dancer, a cup, etc.*)

WENDY: You're givin' your stomach a rest – you might as well give your lungs a rest an' all! (*Semi-laugh.*) So what 'ave you been up to?

NICOLA: Nothin'!

WENDY: Look at the state of you . . . chalk-white face . . . Blimey, you look like a ghost. You'd frighten the birds, you would! (*Laughing*) No wonder you didn't peg me washin' out!

> (*She is very amused by this.* NICOLA *leaves the room.*)
> (*Half to herself*) Oh, never mind, eh? (*She polishes two ceramic shepherdesses, one human, one feline. She carries on with her cleaning. Her amusement has given way to pain.*)

Meanwhile, in the kitchen of the Regret Rien, AUBREY *bears a handful of wet tongues from the cooker to the workbench, where he slaps them down on the slab. His assistant,* PAULA, *stands vacantly by the fridge.*

AUBREY: I was like you. I started at the bottom . . . y'know? I was on the sink for six weeks before I got a look in. It's all about keepin' your eyes peeled. (*He is peeling a tongue.*) These tongues are a pain in the neck. (*He prods it with a knife.*) Can't get into the crevices.

PAULA: Is it a pig's tongue?

AUBREY: Lamb's tongue. Couldn't get a pig's tongue in your mouth. Stick in your throat.

PAULA: Would it?

> (*Pause.*)

AUBREY: You look quite attractive in white. Suits you.
     (*She lowers her eyes. Pause. He twiddles the end of the tongue.*)
     Those are skins – chuck 'em away.
     (*She does so. Then she leans on the workbench.*)
     Good. (*He observes her out of the corner of his eye.*)

*And a little later, they are upstairs in Aubrey's flat. Under his
guidance, PAULA is playing the drums – he is standing behind her,
controlling her by holding her hands, like a puppet.*
     This burst climaxes with a cymbal clash. PAULA looks bewildered.
AUBREY: Hey! You got rhythm . . . y'know? 'Ere, 'ave some
     more.
     (*He holds a glass of red wine to her lips. She takes a sip.*)
     You done really well today.
PAULA: 'Ave I?
AUBREY: Yeah. I'm really pleased with you. You're quite a tasty
     little worker . . . y'know?
     (*He licks his lips, then he leans forward and nibbles her ear.
     They keel over together until she is lying sideways on the big
     drum. He continues to consume her ear. He also feels her breast.
     She remains open-eyed and expressionless.*)

*The next evening, WENDY and ANDY are in their bedroom. ANDY is
combing his hair in the mirror and WENDY, her hair in rollers and
wearing a dressing gown, is draping NATALIE in a white blouse.*
ANDY: That's nice.
WENDY: It's a bit old-fashioned-lookin', though, innit, that one?
ANDY: Black skirt, white blouse, traditional. I like it.
WENDY: Oh, Andy . . . me legs are like jelly-sticks! (*Laughing.*)
     I'm sorry I said I'd do it now! (*She places a black-and-white
     blouse over the white one.*)
NATALIE: Just go for it!
ANDY: You wore that for Joan's wedding, didn't yer?
WENDY: Oh, blimey, yeah! Ah, poor Joan!
     (ANDY *is combing his beard.*)
ANDY: Huh! Poor Donald. (*He laughs.*)
NATALIE: What about Tracey?
     (*Pause.*)
WENDY: I like this . . .

ANDY: Yeah, now you're talking!

WENDY: Yeah – that's the one, innit?

ANDY: Yeah!

(NATALIE *is now draped in a pinky-violet floral blouse.*)

NATALIE: I preferred the white.

WENDY: Oh, blimey . . . I'm gonna be late! (*She puts the three blouses away.*) Oh, eh, Andy – d'you remember this? (*She takes out of the wardrobe a bright-pink angora knitted top, which causes both her and* ANDY *to break out into peals of uncontrollable mirth, although* NATALIE, *on whom* WENDY *again drapes the piece, remains unamused. The hilarity subsides and* WENDY *puts the top away.*)

ANDY: D'you do us any tea, Wen?

WENDY: Yeah, there's a little chicken casserole in the oven.

ANDY: That's nice.

(WENDY *sits at her dressing table.* ANDY *stops by* NATALIE *in the doorway.*)

ANDY: You 'ungry?

NATALIE: 'Ere, I went to this old girl's 'ouse today, right? She 'ad 'er dead dog lyin' on the sofa.

ANDY: She never!

WENDY: Eh?

NATALIE: No, the skin . . . spread out like a rug.

ANDY: Oh, charming.

WENDY: Ugh . . .!

NATALIE: She 'ad arthritic 'ands – couldn't turn 'er tap on. Thought it was bust.

WENDY: Ah . . .

NATALIE: I went straight to it, gave it a good twist an' it was perfectly all right.

ANDY: So what d'you do, then?

NATALIE: Well, I changed the washer for 'er so she didn't look stupid.

WENDY: Oh, that's a good girl! (*She is applying her eye make-up.*)

ANDY: D'you charge 'er a call-out?

NATALIE: Well, I 'ad to – you know what they're like . . . didn't want to.

ANDY: Where was this, then?

NATALIE: Off the A10 somewhere. She said she'd give me some

toffee only she couldn't find 'er ration book.

ANDY: Did she?

WENDY: Oh, bless 'er!

ANDY: Don't suppose you know what a ration book is, do you?

NATALIE: 'Course I do!

ANDY: Meet all sorts in your business, don't you?

NATALIE: And she kept callin' me a 'good lad'!

WENDY: Oh, she never!

NATALIE: Yeah.

WENDY: Well, you should 'ave said to 'er, 'Listen, I'm a miss!' (*She laughs.*)

NATALIE: No – no point.

ANDY: More interesting than my job. Same every day. We 'ad a bloke slice the end off 'is finger this morning.

NATALIE: What, right off?

ANDY: No, there was like a flap . . . (*He demonstrates.*)

WENDY: Ooh! Oh, Andy – don't!

NATALIE: Christ!

ANDY: Lot o' blood. No, it was 'is own fault. I 'ave a very good accident record, as it 'appens.

WENDY: Yeah – we know!

ANDY: No, it's true. It's 'cos I drum it into them: 'Health and Safety! Health and Safety!' Still, you're always going to get someone showing off, in't you?

NATALIE: Yeah.

WENDY: Oh, blimey – I 'aven't done me nails . . .

ANDY: Come on, let's leave 'er in peace. She's got to get ready for 'er big night.
(*They leave.* WENDY *is applying her lipstick.*)

WENDY: And shut the door! (*An apprehensive half-laugh to herself in the mirror.*) Oh, Wendy . . .

Later, at the Regret Rien. WENDY, *now fully dolled up (in a blouse that isn't one of the ones discussed in the previous scene), is standing with* AUBREY, *who is clutching a can of lager.*

AUBREY: You look fantastic, d'you know that, Wendy?

WENDY: Oh, thanks . . . only I didn't want to let you down, you know?

AUBREY: You 'aven't.

WENDY: I've 'ad six different blouses on tonight. No, so long as
     you're 'appy. You know . . .
AUBREY: You're . . . superb! (*He walks abruptly towards the
     kitchen. He is wearing a beret, a vest and a pair of shorts.*)
WENDY: 'Ey, is that what you're wearin'?
     (*He stops.*)
     'Ey, 'Lend us your 'at, we're 'aving' soup!' That's what me
     mum used to say.
     (*She laughs. So does* AUBREY, *mirthlessly. Then he disappears
     into the kitchen.* WENDY *chortles at him and sets about untangling
     some forks.*)

In the kitchen, AUBREY *leans over* PAULA.
AUBREY: You hungry? I'll buy you some fish and chips later,
     y'know?
PAULA: Will yer?
     (*He glances briefly over his shoulder.*)
AUBREY: I might.
     (*Pause. For a moment he hovers, as though he were going to kiss
     her, but he walks out.* PAULA *sighs and sprawls across the worktop.*

A bit later. AUBREY *is now in a smart suit. He and* WENDY *are
standing behind the bar, inspecting his handwritten menu.*

AUBREY: So, you've got tripe soufflé . . .

WENDY: Yeah?

AUBREY: Kidney vol-au-vent . . .

WENDY: Oh, vol-au-vents, yeah . . . we 'ad them on me twenty-first, vol-au-vents – they're nice.

AUBREY: That's with a whole kidney.

WENDY: Ugh!

AUBREY: King prawn in jam sauce . . .

WENDY: Oh, yeah . . . just the one!

AUBREY: Chilled brains . . . they speak for themselves.

WENDY: Oh, not brains.

AUBREY: Prune quiche – that's the one for our vegetarian friends.

WENDY: Right.

AUBREY: Black pudding and Camembert soup –

WENDY: Oh, no, don't!

AUBREY: Boiled bacon consommé –

WENDY: Ah, now, consommé: that's the same as soup, innit?

AUBREY: It's basically the bacon water.

WENDY: Yeah . . . that's like what your mum gives you when you're ill.

AUBREY: And a saveloy on a bed o' lychees.

WENDY: Oh, you got a little Chinesey one in there.

AUBREY: That's all your hors-d'oeuvres, and you're on to your entrées. (*He turns over the sheet of paper.*)

WENDY: Right, so this is me main courses type o' thing, right. What's that one there? Pork what, pork list?

AUBREY: Pork cyst.

WENDY: Cyst?

AUBREY: Yeah.

WENDY: Oh, you're jokin' me!

AUBREY: No.

WENDY: Oh, it's not called cyst!

(*She laughs.* AUBREY *nods.*)

Ah . . . me dad 'ad one o' them.

AUBREY: Did 'e?

WENDY: Yeah . . . underneath.

(*Demonstrating on* AUBREY. *He jumps. She laughs.*)

'Ey – cough! Ah, bless 'im! What is it?

AUBREY: It's like a dumpling – y'know?

WENDY: Oh, I couldn't!

(AUBREY *coughs*.)

AUBREY: And then we 'ave . . . duck in chocolate sauce –

WENDY: Yeah?

AUBREY: Tongues in a rhubarb hollandaise –

WENDY: Ooh, no! (*She laughs.*)

AUBREY: Liver in lager . . .

WENDY: Mmm?

AUBREY: And clams in ham. That's with a pan-fried, cockle-based sauce.

WENDY: Yeah?

AUBREY: Or quails on a bed of spinach with treacle . . .

(WENDY *chuckles*.)

AUBREY: . . . or my *pied de resistance*, grilled trotters with eggs over-easy.

WENDY: Oh, right. What's over-easy? (*She takes the menu*).

AUBREY: Stateside – sunny-side up, y'know.

WENDY: Oh, yeah? I like 'em turned. Oh, blimey, Aubrey, I'll never remember all this!

AUBREY: You'll be fine. Any problems, refer 'em to me.

WENDY: Yeah, but you'll be in the kitchen, cooking, won't you?

AUBREY: Yeah – I'll be in there, I'll be out here, I'll be everywhere. I'll be, er . . . *chef patron*, y'know?

WENDY: Well, you should've 'ad your little menus printed up, like I told you, right?

AUBREY: Yeah, yeah, no sweat. I want this restaurant to be built on a one-to-one, mouth-to-mouth reputation . . . y'know? (*pause*). Would you like a glass of wine, Wendy?

WENDY: Oh, no thanks, no. Me stomach's all of a go with me nerves.

(AUBREY *produces a bottle of red wine and a fresh glass – he already has one.*)

AUBREY: Yeah, go on, it might settle you down.

WENDY: Oh, go on then – just 'alf a glass!

(*He fills both their glasses.*)

WENDY: Oh, by the way, I forgot – I've got something for you!

AUBREY: 'Ave you? Oh, great.

(WENDY *goes to get her handbag. As she takes out an envelope, she realizes that* PAULA *has come into the dining room and is standing by the wall.*)

WENDY: All right?
> (WENDY *returns to the bar.* PAULA *follows.*)

PAULA: I wanna go for a fag.

AUBREY: What?
> (WENDY *looks at her watch.*)
> Now? We're busy!

PAULA: (*Looking round*) Are we?
> (*Pause.*)

AUBREY: Yeah, well, go on then. Be quick. Just have half a one.

WENDY: With a bit o' luck, I'll get me fortune told later! (*She giggles.*)

AUBREY: Feel free.
> (*She laughs.*)

WENDY: Got a little card for you. (*She gives him the envelope.*)

AUBREY: Oh, thanks very much!

WENDY: That's from me and Andy and the girls.

AUBREY: Oh, that's fantastic. (*He takes out the card.*) That's really brilliant, that's really marvellous, you're a really attractive woman. Really – thanks very much. Really. (*He puts the card on the fridge.*)

WENDY: All the best! Good luck.
> (*They raise and touch glasses.*)

AUBREY: Thank you.
> (*He swigs down the whole glassful in one gulp.* WENDY *has a sip. Pause.* AUBREY *looks at his watch, then, suddenly, and shouting:* We are now officially open!!! (*He pushes past* WENDY.)

WENDY: Blimey! Sorry! – Sorry!
> (*Watched by* WENDY *and* PAULA, *who drifts in holding her fag,* AUBREY *rushes to the door and unlocks it. He reverses the 'Open/Closed' sign and closes the inner door.*)

Meanwhile, ANDY *is sitting with* PATSY *at the bar of a crowded pub. They swig their beers intermittently.*

PATSY: As far as I'm concerned, football died the day Arsenal won the double.

ANDY: That's right, yeah.

PATSY: What was they? Workhorses.

ANDY: They were boring buggers, ain't they?

PATSY: Whereas the Spurs double team, they was artists, wasn't they?

ANDY: Yeah, they was artists.

PATSY: Twenty-one quid a week they got – can you imagine? What do they get today? Millions.

ANDY: Then they got the backhanders on top of that, ain't they?

PATSY: Poncing round the penalty area with their 'andbags.

ANDY: Yeah, prima donnas.

PATSY: (*'Pansy' voice*) 'Oh, 'e kicked me, ref!'

(*Pause. They swig their beers.*)

Brown . . . Baker . . .

ANDY: 'Enry.

ANDY/PATSY: Blanchflower.

PATSY: Danny Boy.

ANDY: Yeah.

PATSY: 'E was the architect of the modern game, you know?

ANDY: That's right, yeah, Norman,

ANDY: /PATSY: McKay . . .

PATSY: Jones.

ANDY: Jones –

PATSY: White.

ANDY: Smith.

ANDY/PATSY: Alan, Dyson.

ANDY: Yeah . . . 'Come on, you Spurs!!'

PATSY: John White . . . what a player, eh?

ANDY: Yeah.

PATSY: I used to 'ave a little picture of 'im on my wall.

ANDY: Yeah?

PATSY: Ringed in black.

ANDY: Yeah – tragic.

PATSY: What a way to go!

ANDY: Struck by lightning.

PATSY: On a golf course.

ANDY: What a waste, eh? D'you want another?

PATSY: Yeah, all right.

ANDY: Want something with it?

PATSY: Yeah . . . rum and black.

ANDY: Large one?

PATSY: Yeah, all right.

ANDY: Yeah. (*He glances round for the barman.*)

A bit later, the restaurant is as yet empty and AUBREY *is still behind the bar. He is just uncorking another bottle of wine.* WENDY *is bopping to herself, although there is no music playing.* AUBREY *fills his glass.*

AUBREY: See, the thing is . . . is that people don't like to venture out too early, do they?

WENDY: No, not on a Tuesday, no.

AUBREY: No, they like to get home, have a bath, chill out, have their tea . . . and then go out to eat.

WENDY: Did you put an advert in the paper?

AUBREY: Mm . . . yeah, yeah . . . yeah, yeah – yeah. (*Pause.*) No, I didn't, actually.

WENDY: You should have 'ad some little cards printed then. I could've given 'em out in the shop.

AUBREY: Yeah, well, I didn't want to attract the wrong sort of people, y'know?

WENDY: (*Laughing*) Oh, charming! Oh, thanks very much, Aubrey.

AUBREY: Would you like another glass of wine, Wendy?

WENDY: Oh, yeah, go on, all right. I'll keep you company.
    (*She crosses to the bar with her glass, which she holds while he fills it.*)

AUBREY: Great hands!
    (*She laughs and moves slightly away. He tops up his glass.*)

At the same moment, NATALIE *and* NICOLA *are sitting in their living room.*

NATALIE: D'you think you'll ever 'ave kids?

NICOLA: No!

NATALIE: Well, you're pretty sure for one so young.

NICOLA: What, and look like a tank for nine months? Gimme a break!

NATALIE: Well, is that all you're worried about, what you'll look like?

NICOLA: I'd make a good mother.

NATALIE: Oh, would you?

NICOLA: Yeah.
    (*Pause.*)

Why – d'you want kids?

NATALIE: Yeah . . . in the fullness of time.

NICOLA: Do you?

NATALIE: 'Course.

NICOLA: You've got to 'ave a boyfriend first.

NATALIE: Yeah, one does generally need a bloke – this is true.

NICOLA: Well, you're not doing very well, then, are you?

NATALIE: Well, I 'aven't seen your men exactly queuing up in droves.

NICOLA: You don't know.

NATALIE: What, they sneak around 'ere in the daytime, do they, when no one's in?

NICOLA: Anyway, you don't need a bloke to 'ave a kid.

NATALIE: Well, I wouldn't fancy bringing one up on me own.

NICOLA: Well, it's better to be on your own than be with a bastard.

NATALIE: Well, presumably you wouldn't choose a bastard in the first place, if you 'ad any sense.

NICOLA: All men are bastards!

NATALIE: What?!

NICOLA: They're all potential rapists.

NATALIE: That's a bit sweepin'!

NICOLA: All men have got the ability to rape.

NATALIE: Well, they don't all do it, do they?

NICOLA: If they've got the ability, they've got the desire.

NATALIE: That's paranoid rubbish!

NICOLA: What d'you know about paranoia?

NATALIE: Well, not 'alf as much as you do, I'll give you that.

NICOLA: You'll find out when you get to America.

NATALIE: I'm only going on a holiday!

NICOLA: So?

NATALIE: What, you think I'm gonna get yanked off the plane at John F. Kennedy airport, and be raped and pillaged, do you?

NICOLA: You've got to be on your guard.

NATALIE: D'you 'ear what I just said?

NICOLA: What?

NATALIE: 'Yanked.' Get it?

NICOLA: What?

NATALIE: Yanked . . . America.

NICOLA: Racist!

(*She gets up and walks out of the room.*)

Back at the still-empty restaurant, AUBREY *is standing on a chair, looking out of the window. He clutches the bottle and the glass. He is now fairly drunk.*

AUBREY: There's another bloody couple coming. Yeah! Yeah – they're coming this way . . . Definitely.

(WENDY *is leaning behind the counter. She is bored.*)

WENDY: D'you want me to tell Paula again?

AUBREY: Yeah . . . ACTION STATIONS!!

(WENDY *starts for the kitchen door.*)

No . . . shit! Fucking yuppies!

(*He empties his glass and pours some more.* WENDY *returns to the bar from the kitchen door, having had a look through its window.* AUBREY *staggers across towards her, unsteadily grunting. He arrives at the bar and puts down the bottle.*)

They went straight past.

WENDY: Oh, did they? Well, perhaps they weren't 'ungry.

AUBREY: Where's Pauline?

WENDY: She's sittin' on your work-surface.

AUBREY: Is she?

WENDY: Yeah, she's picking.

AUBREY: Right . . .

(*She watches him go to the kitchen door and fail to open it. Then he realizes he's been pushing at the wrong side and he goes in. Left alone,* WENDY *looks very fed up indeed.*)

In the kitchen, PAULA *is sitting on the worktop, indeed picking at her foot.* AUBREY *passes her and goes towards the cooker.*

AUBREY: Don't sit up there, Pauline. It's unhygienic. Cross-infection.

(*She gets down and leans on the worktop.*)

These stocks are reducing nicely. (*He stirs one.*) The secret of a great sauce . . . is a well-reduced stock. No stock, no sauce. (*He throws the spoon in the sink.*) Key to the door.

(*He comes over to* PAULA. *She backs up against the fridge. He leans over her.*)

You're working with a genius. D'you know that? I'm not just a wanker . . . y'know! I could teach you things . . . you never even dreamed of. I'm a magician.

PAULA: I want a drink.

(*He opens the fridge a little.*)

AUBREY: There's plenty of orange juice in there – help yourself.

(*He closes the fridge with a jolt.*)

PAULA: I want some wine.

AUBREY: I can't 'ave you gettin' drunk. Kitchen's a very dangerous place.

PAULA: She's got wine.

(AUBREY *grunts a knowing laugh.*)

AUBREY: Me and Wendy . . . we go back a long way – y'know? I'm an old friend of the family. (*He studies her at close range, then he runs his finger down her nose and taps it abruptly on the end.*) Classic nose.

(*He takes a swig of wine, then holds up the glass and examines it. Then he belches.*) 'Ere . . .

(*He gives her the glass and squeezes obscenely past her. Alone, she gazes down at the mouthful of wine at the bottom of the glass.*)

ANDY *and* PATSY *are still at the bar. Both are now extremely drunk.* PATSY *produces something from a carrier bag.*

PATSY: 'Ere. 'Ave you seen this?

ANDY: What you got there? Oh, let's 'ave a look. Pocket telly!

PATSY: Yeah.

ANDY: Can I 'ave a butcher's?

PATSY: Feel free.

(ANDY *gets it out of its box.*)

ANDY: It's good, innit?

PATSY: Yeah – neat.

ANDY: Let's 'ave a go. (*He extends the aerial.*)

PATSY: Leave it out! You prannit!

(*He retracts the aerial, whilst* ANDY *seeks to demonstrate the thing to somebody behind them.*)

ANDY: 'Ey, seen these?

PATSY: Give us it, give us it back. (*He retrieves it.*)

ANDY: 'Ow much d'you want for that, then.

PATSY: Well, I could . . . let you 'ave it 'alf-price. A hundred nicker.

ANDY: Nice, innit?

PATSY: Yeah . . . be tasty on the salad wagon. Wouldn't it?

ANDY: No . . . can't afford it. (*He swigs some beer.*)

PATSY: What about that 'undred?

ANDY: What 'undred?

PATSY: That 'undred you never gave me.

ANDY: You know . . . if someone 'ad turned up with that twenty-five . . . years ago . . . and said they were a bloody Martian, you'd 'ave 'ad to believe 'em, wouldn't you?

(PATSY *puts it back in its box.*)

PATSY: Yeah, yeah. So, you don't want it?

ANDY: No, Patsy, I don't want it. I don't want anything. (*He takes another swig.*)

PATSY: Mean bastard!

(PATSY *bends down to reach the bag, which is on the floor. But he overbalances and falls off his stool.* ANDY *looks down at him in alarm. A young couple glance at him in passing.*)

Whilst AUBREY *bursts out of the Regret Rien into the empty late-night street, bottle in hand, guffawing with bitter laughter. He hollers at the world . . .*

AUBREY: Come on, you bastards!! I'm open!! I'm ready, I'm waitin' for you – this is what you've all been waitin' for! Come and get it!! Fishwives! Footballers! You English dickheads! You can stick to your fish and chips – go on, go and get cancer!

(WENDY *comes out.*)

Thousand pounds! Ten thousand pounds!

(*She tries to pull him inside.*)

WENDY: Aubrey . . . Aubrey, stop shouting, right?

AUBREY: Gourmet cookin'!

WENDY: Stop shouting!

AUBREY: You working-class morons! Go and eat your own shit – go on, go on!

(WENDY *manages to get him inside, where, a few seconds later, she wrests the bottle from his grip.*)

WENDY: That is enough . . . no more. Right? 'Cos you're being a naughty boy!

(*He throws his arms round her.*)

AUBREY: Marry me, Wendy.

WENDY: What?

AUBREY: I wanna marry you. (*He tries to kiss her neck.*)

WENDY: Now, stop it! Aubrey, stop it – get off!
(*She smacks him lightly. As he releases his grip, his spectacles fall off.* WENDY *rescues them.*)

AUBREY: I love you. Y'know?

WENDY: Now don't be stupid, right? I'm already married – I'm married to Andy.

AUBREY: I love Andy . . . he's my best friend.

WENDY: Yeah, well, we're very fond of you – now you know that.
(*He shakes her.*)

AUBREY: I don't care! – I don't care if you're married to Andy! You can still marry me. You don't – you don't 'ave to tell 'im.

WENDY: Now stop it. Right? – now sit down! (*She positions a chair.*) Sit down.
(*He leans on her.*)
What're you doing? Get off me! Aubrey, stop it now!
(*He hugs her again.*)

AUBREY: I wanna fuck you, Wendy.

WENDY: Now stop talkin' like that. Now just stop it, right, because Andy won't let me come 'ere again – d'y'ear me? 'E won't!
(*Still hanging on to her, he has dropped to the floor.*)

AUBREY: I worship the ground . . . you walk on.

WENDY: Now look, you're bendin' down – that means you're gonna be sick.

AUBREY: I kiss your feet. (*He does so.*)

WENDY: Well, there might be a little bit o' doggy on me shoes, right? – and you're not gonna like that, so get up!
(*She tries to pull him up. He gets up anyhow, still clutching her.*)

AUBREY: Nicola!

WENDY: What?

AUBREY: Oh, Nicola . . .

WENDY: Nicola's not 'ere, right? She's at home. Saving the world. Now look. You've got vodka all down your suit. And that's your best suit you bought for tonight, right?

AUBREY: It's all right . . .

WENDY: Sit down.

AUBREY: I don't wannit, I, I don't wannit.

WENDY: What? Sit down.

(*He takes off his jacket.*)

AUBREY: I want Andy to have it.

WENDY: Andy doesn't wannit.

AUBREY: Yeah, he's a poor man!

WENDY: Andy's got a suit.

AUBREY: No, 'e can wear it in the fuckin' stupid caravan s –

WENDY: Now, stop that!

AUBREY: Stupid fuckin' . . . (*He sits down.*)

WENDY: Behave yourself!

AUBREY: 'E can 'ave the suit 'cos 'e's more scruffy than me, 'e's
. . . (*He starts undoing his trousers.*)

WENDY: What're you doin'?

AUBREY: I'm gonna give 'im the suit.

WENDY: Leave your trousers on, Aubrey! Aubrey, leave your
trousers on!

(*But they are off.*)

Behave yourself and leave your trousers on.

AUBREY: Give 'im my suit . . . I love him and . . . Give 'em to
him.

WENDY: I'll tell you what . . .

(*She gathers up the trousers.* AUBREY *is staggering about.*)

What're you doing now? You're gonna fall!

AUBREY: No, I'm not drunk! Right? I'm not drunk! (*He upturns a
fully laden table against the wall. Much noise of breakage.*)

WENDY: Now . . . behave yourself, right? You're being silly!

(*He upturns another table.*)

Aubrey! Aubrey, will you stop it?!!

(*He lurches forward.*)

AUBREY: No . . .

WENDY: Now you're behaving like an idiot – listen to me!

AUBREY: No regrets . . .

WENDY: No . . . you don't do any more – no!

AUBREY: No regrets, *rien*!

WENDY: Now stop it – Aubrey!!

(*He removes the cloth from yet another fully laden table and
drapes it over his head.*)

AUBREY: No regrets . . .

(*Wrapped in the cloth, he staggers to the wall and tears down the Piaf portrait and a string of garlic.* WENDY *rushes past him. He lurches forward and, tearing down a birdcage, he smashes it to the floor and staggers about.*)

WENDY *emerges from the kitchen cautiously, with* PAULA. *Both watch as* AUBREY *finally collapses on the floor on his back, spark out in his shirt and striped underpants.*
   Pause.

WENDY: Blimey. Shame though, innit? Come on, Paula, we're goin'. (*Pause.*) Oh, look at me. (*She's holding his trousers. She puts them down.*) Well, that's all right – he'll find 'em there in the morning. Oh, what a night! (*She puts on her coat.*) I'll tell you what . . . Never again. What a mistake. (*Pause.*) It's all right – he's only asleep. (*Laughing.*) He's not dead . . . there's no need to be frightened!

PAULA: I'm not frightened.

WENDY: Heh?

PAULA: There's nowt to be frightened of.

WENDY: All right. Is this your little coat? (*She takes it down, with a bag.*) 'Ere's your bag. Now, 'ow are you getting 'ome? Heh?

PAULA: Bus.

WENDY: Right – got your fare? Where's your little purse? In 'ere? (*Tapping the bag.*) Where's your cigarettes?

PAULA: In me pocket.

WENDY: Right, come on then!
   (PAULA *moves away from her, sulkily.*)
   What's the matter? Eh?

PAULA: We're goin' for chips.

WENDY: Who's going for chips?

PAULA: Me and Aubrey.

WENDY: Aubrey's in a coma, he doesn't want any chips.

PAULA: Well, he'll be 'ungry when 'e wakes up, won't 'e? Stands to reason.

WENDY: All right, I'll buy you chips.

PAULA: I don't want no chips.

WENDY: All right, well I won't buy you chips. Come on, Paula. Look, I tell you what – take your hat off . . . (*She removes*

68

Paula's kerchief.) . . . put your coat on – we don't want to frighten people, do we? (*She laughs.*)

(*Their attention is attracted by a loud snoring grunt from the sweating* AUBREY.)

AUBREY: (*Kissing his hand*) Nicola . . .

WENDY: Oh, blimey, 'ark at him! Look, I tell you what . . . I'll run you to the bus stop – OK? (*Pause.*) Paula . . . Are you coming with me?

PAULA: I'm stoppin' 'ere.

WENDY: You can't stop 'ere.

(AUBREY *snores loudly.*)

Please, Paula . . . Come on . . .

WENDY *is in her car. She pulls up outside her house.*

WENDY: Blinkin' 'eck! (*She walks up to the front door. She turns towards the streetlight, so that she can find her keys in her bag. Suddenly she gasps with horror – a pair of feet are sticking out of the caravan. Cautiously, she creeps towards them, then she looks into the caravan.*) Andy!

(*He is lying, perhaps dead, on the floor.*)

Andy!

(*He wakes up and raises his head.*)

ANDY: What?

WENDY: Oh, blimey, what're you doin'?

ANDY: Hmm? I'm tidyin' up.

Minutes later, just inside the front door. WENDY *is struggling with a very drunken* ANDY. *He wants to go to the kitchen, but* WENDY, *with a bit of help from* NATALIE, *is trying to steer him upstairs.*

WENDY: You're not 'aving no lager!

ANDY: Get us a lager, Nat.

NATALIE: You must be jokin'.

WENDY: You've 'ad enough lager for tonight, right? – bloomin' lager lout. Now get up the stairs!

(*In the struggle,* ANDY *has accidentally knocked the tubular bells, which are chiming.*)

What're you doin'?

(*He is trying to get to the door.*)

ANDY: Somebody at the door.

WENDY: There's nobody at the door – that's you! Listen, you'll 'ave Eileen bangin' on the wall again, and you won't like that.

ANDY: (*Through the door*) What d'you want? 'Oo is it?

NATALIE: Come on, Dad!

ANDY: Where's the lager?

NATALIE: In the fridge.

WENDY: Get up the stairs.

ANDY: Yeah, all right, all right!

(*He proceeds up the stairs on* NATALIE'S *arm.* NICOLA *appears from the living room and watches.*)

WENDY: Look at the state of you! You've got your best trousers on, you've got your new shoes . . .

(*He stops.*)

Blime – now what? What're you doin'?

ANDY: I'm gonna shut the caravan door.

WENDY: I've shut the caravan door!

NICOLA: Is 'e gonna be sick? (*She disappears into the room.*)

WENDY: Don't you be sick on me, Andy!

ANDY: Nicola, shut the caravan door!

NICOLA: (*Reappearing*) No!

(ANDY *and* NATALIE *continue upstairs.*)

NATALIE: Come on, let's get you 'orizontal.

(WENDY *pushes him from behind.*)

WENDY: Oh, shit your carcass, come on!

ANDY: Brown, Baker, 'Enry . . .

NATALIE: How'd it go tonight?

ANDY: Mackay . . . Blanchflower . . .

WENDY: Terrible, if you must know.

NATALIE: Why?

WENDY: Tell you later – no, Andy, no! Get in that toilet, and do a wee. (*She pushes him into the toilet, instead of the bedroom, where he was aiming.*) Oh, blimey! Look . . . lift the seat – I don't want me carpet all soaking wet! (*She puts on the toilet light.*) And close the door! (*She closes it.*) You've got two daughters. What's the matter with you?

ANDY: (*From inside*) That's what's the matter with me – I've got two daughters.

WENDY: Oh, shut up!

(NATALIE *and* NICOLA *are standing together at the top of the stairs.*)

NICOLA: What did I tell you?

NATALIE: So come on, then. What 'appened at the restaurant?

NICOLA: 'Ow many tips did you score?

WENDY: Nothing 'appened at the restaurant, right? And keep it out! (*Points to nose.*) I've had enough for one night! I'm up to 'ere with the lot of you!!
(*She goes into her bedroom and slams the door. The twins exchange a glance and return downstairs.*)

Early next morning. The start of a sunny day and the birds are chirruping. A high-angle shot: we pan along the row of houses with their back gardens, ending on Wendy and Andy's.

Inside, WENDY *is sitting up in bed with a mug of tea.* ANDY *sits on the end of the bed, fixing his tie.*

WENDY: 'Ey, 'e could be dead this morning, you know, Andy? I'm not kiddin'. All that broken glass, 'e might've severed an artery. Should've called the police, shouldn't I?

ANDY: I feel like Princess Margaret.

WENDY: I could've killed you last night.

ANDY: I'll drop in on 'im on me way back from work. Tell him 'e was out of order.

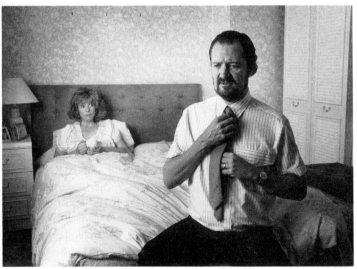

WENDY: Will you?

ANDY: Yeah.

WENDY: I suppose I've lost me 'undred quid now, 'aven't I?

ANDY: I'll get it off 'im . . . he's not going to get away with that. Outrageous behaviour. I gotta go, Wen. (*He goes over and kisses her.*)

WENDY: See you tonight.

ANDY: Yeah. I'll be late.

WENDY: Where you going? (*He is putting on his jacket.*)

ANDY: I'm meeting Patsy for a drink.

WENDY: You're not!!

ANDY: Got you!!

(*They both laugh.*)

(*Hangover*) Ooh!

WENDY: Get out.

(*With a look that expresses how delicate he feels, he goes. She chortles and then snuggles down in the bed with her tea. The front door slams. For a moment she listens for* NICOLA, *then she closes her eyes.*)

Later that day. The blue Ford Escort is parked outside the house. A stout youth ambles past.

Inside, in the living room, NICOLA *is kneeling on top of her* LOVER. *They are kissing.*

NICOLA: Come on, let's go up.

LOVER: No.

NICOLA: What?

LOVER: Not yet.

NICOLA: I know you want it.

LOVER: (*Amused*) Do I?

NICOLA: Yeah.

LOVER: 'Ow do you know?

NICOLA: Synchronicity.

(*He laughs and imitates Donald Duck.*)

Shut up!

LOVER: I don't want *it*.

NICOLA: What d'you mean?

LOVER: I want . . . *you*.

NICOLA: Sentimentalist.

LOVER: No, no, no – I come in, we go straight upstairs, we do it
. . . Bingo! You're a pain in the arse – I don't want that, I
want to see you nice.

NICOLA: What's nice? Only a boring cliché.
(*She goes to kiss him. He turns away.*)

LOVER: No – nice, nice – showing me a bit of civility, a bit of
respect.

NICOLA: You don't show me no respect!

LOVER: I'm tryin' to respect you now, tryin' to treat you like a
real person instead of some fuckin' shagbag. (*Pause.*) Come
on, talk to me.

NICOLA: What about? (*She leans away from him.*)

LOVER: Anything! Anything you think, anything you know . . .
What d'you care about?

NICOLA: Eh?

LOVER: You got all these fucking books upstairs, your *Women
Who Love Men Too Much, Men Who Hate Women, Women
Who Love, Women in Love, Women's Room, Female Eunuch*
. . . Have you – have you read any of that crap?

NICOLA: What's it to you?

LOVER: 'Ave you?

NICOLA:'Course.

LOVER: So what 'ave you learnt from it?
    (*Pause.*)
NICOLA: That I'm a feminist.
LOVER: What's a 'feminist'?
    (*She puts her arms round him.*)
NICOLA: Oh, come on . . .
LOVER: No, no, no – what's it mean?
NICOLA: Stop bein' antagonistic.
LOVER: I'm not bein' antagonistic. I'm trying to 'ave an
    intelligent conversation with you. Are you capable of that?
    Eh?
    (*Pause. She has sat back again.*)
    I don't think you are, are you? Really. Bit . . . vacant, ain't
    you? Bit of an air-'ead. Nothing goin' on; bit dumb; but
    dizzy; dimbo-bimbo, dumb blonde stuff – in't ya, eh? (*He
    taps her on the head aggressively.*) 'Allo – anyone at home?
    'Allo? 'Allo?! (*Pause.*) You're a fake.
    (*Pause. She is shaken. Her fingers twitch on her cheeks.*)
NICOLA: I am intelligent. Are you comin' upstairs?
    (*Pause.*)
LOVER: No.
NICOLA: Well, piss off, then!
LOVER: All right!
    (*He extracts himself from under her, gets his jacket and leaves.
    The front door slams.*)

That afternoon. WENDY *is walking home from work, carrying her
shopping. She passes a large street-hoarding – an advert for a bank: a
row of howling babies in cots.*

In Nicola's bedroom, WENDY *is gathering up the vacuum cleaner.*
NICOLA *is sitting on her bed, hugging a pillow and smoking a fag.*
WENDY: Blimey days, Nicola – look at the state of you. You're
    sittin' there like there's a grey cloud over you, it's like the
    sun's gone in. You've got no energy 'cos you don't eat your
    dinners. And you've got no joy in your soul.
NICOLA: 'Ow do you know?
WENDY: I know, because you've given up. 'Cos you're not 'appy,
    that's 'ow I know. (*She takes the vacuum cleaner out on to the*

74

landing.)

NICOLA: I am happy.

WENDY: You've lost all your friends. I don't see them knockin' on the door any more.

NICOLA: I don't want friends. They disappoint you.

WENDY: I mean, you say you wanna change the world – you're supposed to be political, but I don't see you doin' anything about it.

NICOLA: I am political. And shut the door.

(*She stubs out her fag.* WENDY *comes to the doorway.*)

WENDY: How are you political?

NICOLA: I read the paper, I watch the news. I'm more political than you.

WENDY: Oh, blimey, Nicola, we can all watch the telly. You should be out there, 'elping the Old Age Pensioners or goin' on marches or whatever.

NICOLA: Marching's a waste of time. It's boring.

WENDY: If you put your money where your mouth is, you should be joining one of these Socialist . . . whatsit groups, or the Nuclear Disarmament whatever, but you don't. All you do is sit 'ere in this room, starin' at the walls, and tweakin' and twitchin'. (*She makes to go, closing the door almost completely.*)

NICOLA: And you're so perfect!

(*Pause.* WENDY *opens the door again and leans on the frame.*)

WENDY: No . . . I'm not perfect, but I 'aven't given up. I'm still out there, fightin'. And I tell you what, Nicola . . . Every time I look out that window and I see that rusty old caravan sittin' there, do you know what it says to me? It says to me there's a man who 'asn't given up either, who's still out there fightin', lookin' for his dream.

NICOLA: Well, it says to me, there's a man who's gettin' greedy.

WENDY: Greedy? Your dad? 'E's the most unselfish man I've ever met. D'you know, he's up at six o'clock every mornin', sloggin' 'is guts out in a job he 'ates – which is more than you do. And 'e still comes home at the end of the week with sod all.

NICOLA: I'm not prepared to be exploited.

WENDY: Exploited? You're not prepared to work, full stop.

NICOLA: You've accepted Nat as a plumber, and you didn't like

75

that at first.

WENDY: No, I didn't; I didn't like it. But I can see now I was wrong, because she's happy.

NICOLA: I don't know what I want to do, yet.

WENDY: Oh, don't you? Well, you 'ad your chance, Nicola, when you were seventeen, when you were at the college doin' your three A-levels. You were goin' great, and then suddenly you stopped. You stopped eatin', you stopped everything – you ended up eight weeks in the 'ospital.

NICOLA: Well, you put me there – I didn't wanna go.

WENDY: Oh, for God's sake, Nicola, you were at death's door.

NICOLA: You were trying to control my life!

WENDY: You were dying!

NICOLA: No, I wasn't.

WENDY: Yes, you were!

NICOLA: I'd know if I was dying!

WENDY: Dr Harris told us, you had two weeks to live!!

(*Pause.* NICOLA *is shaken by this news.*)

You didn't know that, did you? The three of us, comin' 'ome every night, cryin' our eyes out. You were lucky. Life's not easy, Nicola. I could've given up, right? Sixteen, I was doin' me A-levels.

NICOLA: What A-levels?

WENDY: English and Business Studies, if you must know. And then I got pregnant with twins.

NICOLA: Well, why didn't you 'ave an abortion?

WENDY: Because I didn't want one, because I 'ad two little lives growin' inside me. I don't believe in it – that's the easy way out. Your dad was only seventeen. 'E was at catering college, and he was workin' in hotels at night, tryin' to get a bit extra. We got a little flat together; begged and borrowed – couple o' cots. And when the two of you were born, we were thrilled to bits. Because we 'ad two lovely little babies. We came through, laughin'.

NICOLA: Well, don't blame me! I didn't ask to be born!

WENDY: I'm not blamin' you, Nicola. I just want you to be happy, that's all, and you're not. I wouldn't care what bloomin' job you did, I wouldn't care 'ow scruffy you looked, as long as you were happy. But you're not.

76

Something inside you's died. You've given up. And if one day I could just walk through that door, and you could look at me and you could say, 'Look, Mum, help me, please – I don't know what I'm doin', I don't know where I'm goin' . . .' Then I'd say, 'Great, because now we can be honest with each other. Now we can start talkin'.'

NICOLA: But I'm not in a mess.

WENDY: Aren't you?

NICOLA: You're givin' me a problem when I 'aven't got one.

WENDY: Christ, Nicola . . .

(*Pause.*)

NICOLA: If you 'ate me so much, why don't you throw me out?

WENDY: We don't hate you. We love you, right? You stupid girl!

(*She goes out, closing the door.* NICOLA *sobs uncontrollably. Whilst downstairs in the living room,* WENDY *is also having a quiet cry.*)

During the preceding scene, tears have gradually welled up within both NICOLA *and* WENDY, *eventually surfacing.*

Meanwhile, ANDY *is striding with great authority through his kitchen, carrying a tray of food.*

Suddenly, he steps on a serving spoon and falls over, howling with pain. The tray goes flying and food lands everywhere.

Another CHEF *materializes immediately.*

CHEF: What've you done, you silly sod?

ANDY: I think I've broke my ankle . . . Jeez–! (*He is howling with pain.*)

CHEF: Well, don't touch it – lay flat. Relax! Breathe! Breathe! (*He tries to push* ANDY *into a lying position.*)

ANDY: I am breathing, for Christ's – !

CHEF: Lay flat – relax! Lie there . . . I'll be back.

(*He goes.* ANDY *tries to sit up.*)

ANDY: Neil! Where are you going? Neil! Neil! (*He looks round and spots something near him.*) It's a spoon . . . it's a fucking spoon, for . . . Christ's sake! (*He crawls towards it and picks it up. His chef's hat falls off. He strikes the floor angrily with the spoon.*)

Who dropped this spoon? Who dropped this spoon?!!

A little while later, WENDY *is still standing alone in her living room.*
  The phone rings. She wipes her nose with her handkerchief, picks up the receiver and clears her throat.
WENDY: Hallo? Yeah, speakin', yeah. Oh, hallo, how are you? Oh, blimey, you're jokin' me, 'e 'asn't? Oh, 'ow did 'e do it? (*She burst out laughing.*) Oh, no, I'm sorry, Brian, I'm sorry – I know I shouldn't laugh, but . . . ah, is 'e all right, though? Yeah – no, it's all right, no, I can come over – Yeah. Straight away. All right, thanks for phoning me. Ah . . . yeah, and you. All right, then. Yeah – tat-ta, 'bye! (*She hangs up and reflects for a moment, then –*) Nicola! (*She takes off her apron and goes.*)

Upstairs, NICOLA *lies on her bed, crying.*

Later. A pleasant summer's evening. The car is outside the house.
NATALIE *opens the front passenger door for* ANDY. *He is holding a pair of crutches.* WENDY *is getting a Woolworth's carrier bag from the back seat.*
NATALIE: Oh, Christ!
ANDY: Hello, Nat.
WENDY: State of him. (*She closes the rear door.*) 'Ere y'are – take the bag.
  (NATALIE *takes it.*)
ANDY: Take these, Wen.
WENDY: 'Ere y'are, yeah. (*She takes his crutches.*) Go on . . . 'ow are you gonna do it?
ANDY: Don't know.
WENDY: Oh, blimey . . .
ANDY: 'Ang on, 'ang on . . .
WENDY: Take it steady . . . Ooh!
  (*He eases his right leg out of the car. It is in plaster from his knee to his ankle.*)
ANDY: Ooh-hoo-hoo . . .!! Don't let that door slam!
NATALIE: Don't worry – I've got it!
ANDY: Right, here we –
WENDY: D'you wanna hand?
ANDY: No, no, I'll do it myself. (*He stands up.*)

WENDY: OK?
ANDY: Yeah, yeah.
WENDY: Yeah? Right. There you go. (*She gives him the crutches.*)
ANDY: Give us those. That's it, that's it.
WENDY: Right . . .
ANDY: Yeah, yeah.
WENDY: Take it easy . . . I've got you.
    (*She is holding his arm. They set off.*)
ANDY: All right. 'T's all right. Open the gate, Nat.
NATALIE: Yeah, hold on.
    (NATALIE *and* WENDY *close the car door.*)
ANDY: Go on!
    (NATALIE *holds the gate open.*)
WENDY: Now don't rush, Andy, right?
ANDY: All right. (*He grunts in pain a little.*)
WENDY: Just take it steady. Andy, what're you doin'? Blimey,
    you're not a greyhound in a race!
    (*They go into the house.* NATALIE *closes the gate.*)

Moments later, in the living room. ANDY *is balancing on his good leg.*
NATALIE *is holding one of his crutches and* WENDY *is trying to relieve*
him of the other, but his sleeve is caught in it.
ANDY: Well, take it, Wen!
WENDY: I'm tryin', Andy.
ANDY: Well, get rid of it! (*He wrests his arm free and sinks into an*
    armchair.)
WENDY: All right?
ANDY: Yep.
WENDY: 'E needs a little . . . doofer, dun' 'e?
NATALIE: 'Old on, I'll get this table.
WENDY: Oh, that's it, Nat. (*She picks up a cushion.*)
NATALIE: There we are. (*She carries over a small side-table.*)
WENDY: Right.
NATALIE: That's the job.
    (WENDY *places the cushion on the table.*)
WENDY: Careful, careful, careful . . . Ah . . . (*He eases his leg on to*
    the table.)
WENDY: (*Laughs*) Looks like the Royal Leg. Ah! Look at his little
    face. Ah, poor Andy! Ah . . . 'E's been through a lot, you

know. Hey, listen, how are you going to get your trousers off?

ANDY: Cut 'em.

WENDY: Oh, I'll tell you what – I'll get me little pinkin' shears, right? And I'll come up the inside leg.
(*She mimes this and laughs. He giggles.*)

ANDY: Don't make me laugh, Wen!

WENDY: Ah . . .

NATALIE: How long have you got to have this on for, then?

ANDY: I don't know . . . six or eight weeks, something like that.

NATALIE: Cushy number!

WENDY: Yeah, I wouldn't mind six weeks' 'oliday (*She puts a cushion behind his back.*)

ANDY: No, it's a damned nuisance, as a matter of fact. I was going to get started on the caravan when I got back from work this evening – it's a pisser.

WENDY: Oh, blimey! What about Aubrey?

ANDY: Oh, yeah . . .

NATALIE: What about Aubrey?

WENDY: Oh, let's leave it . . . let 'im stew in his own juice – I've got enough on me plate.

ANDY: Yeah.

NATALIE: Ain't you going in tonight, then?

WENDY: No.

NATALIE: Why?

WENDY: Because. (*Points to nose.*)

ANDY: Where's Nicola?

NATALIE: Upstairs. (*She sits on the sofa.*)

ANDY: Doesn't she know I 'ad an accident?

NATALIE: She told me.

ANDY: Nicola!
(WENDY *picks up the Woolworth's bag.*)

WENDY: 'Ere, I'll 'ang these things up, Andy.

ANDY: No, 'ang on, give us that.

WENDY: What?

ANDY: Give us it 'ere.

WENDY: (*Laughing*) I know what you want! You want your little souvenir, don't you? (*She produces the serving-spoon from the bag.*)

ANDY: Yeah, that's the bastard, that's the culprit!

NATALIE: What?

WENDY: Yeah, tryin' to kid us he slipped on a spoon! 'E was still bloomin' drunk from last night!

(*She goes out.* ANDY *raises the spoon at her in mock anger.*)

NATALIE: Fibber!

ANDY: I've never known pain like it, Nat.

NATALIE: Ain't you?

ANDY: Searing pain.

NATALIE: D'you 'ear it snap?

ANDY: No, I didn't, actually . . . Maybe I did . . . Yeah, I did.

NATALIE: Did you?

ANDY: Yeah. It's like when you break a dry stick across your knee. (*Demonstrates.*) Know what I mean? (*Pause. He groans.*)

Upstairs, WENDY *knocks gently on Nicola's door.*

WENDY: Nicola.

NICOLA: (*Inside*) What?

WENDY: Can I come in?

Back downstairs, ANDY *is examining the spoon.*

ANDY: Look at that. An ordinary spoon. I never noticed it before. There you are . . . 1975. This spoon was born when you were seven years old.

NATALIE: Oh, yeah!

ANDY: It just sits in a drawer. Out of the drawer . . . Into the peas . . . (*Mimes stirring.*) . . . Stir the custard . . . (*Mimes.*) . . . Into the wash, out o' the wash . . . (*Mimes.*) . . . Up on the hooks with all the other spoons . . . (*Mimes.*) . . . And all the time, just waiting for the fatal day when it'd drastically alter the course of a man's life.

NATALIE: Doesn't look dangerous, does it?

ANDY: Nah, you take my word for it – that is an evil spoon.

(NATALIE *takes the spoon.*)

NATALIE: Here y'are, look, put it in a place of honour. Keep an eye on it. (*She hangs it on a framed Degas ballet reproduction on the wall.*)

ANDY: Yeah. I don't trust it.

(NATALIE *sits down again.*)
Get us some chocolate.

Meanwhile, WENDY *is sitting on Nicola's bed with her arm round
her. They talk quietly, intimately.*
WENDY: Tell you what . . . go and give your face a little wash,
    make you feel a bit better, eh?
NICOLA: No.
WENDY: You don't want your dad to know you've been sittin' 'ere
    crying, do you?
NICOLA: 'E don't want to see me.
WENDY: 'E does.
NICOLA: I'll make 'im feel worse.
WENDY: Don't be so daft.
NICOLA: I'm a burden to you.
WENDY: Listen. We gotta turn over a new leaf, yeah? Both of us.
    All of us. Come on, 'ave a little cuppa tea.
NICOLA: No . . . I don't want one.
WENDY: Come on – do it for your dad. 'E's been asking for you.
NICOLA: Has 'e?
WENDY: Yeah. Sittin' there with his tongue hangin' out. You
    know what 'e's like – 'e wants a bit of tea and sympathy.
NICOLA: I just want to talk to you.
WENDY: (*Whispering*) Do you?
    (NICOLA *nods.* WENDY *hugs her. They sway together gently.
    Then* WENDY *kisses Nicola's hair.*)

A little later, NATALIE *emerges from the kitchen into the living room,
holding four tea-mugs.* WENDY *follows her out.*
WENDY: D'you want a 'and, Nat?
NATALIE: No, 't's all right.
WENDY: 'Ere y'are, Andy – gis a little bit of chocolate. Don't 'og
    it all.
ANDY: It's all right. Plenty for everyone. (*From his chair he hands
    her the block of chocolate.*)
WENDY: Ta! 'Ere y'are, Nic . . . want a bit?
    (NICOLA *is sitting on the sofa.*)
NICOLA: No . . .
NATALIE: Here y'are, Dad. (*She gives* ANDY *his tea.*)

WENDY: Go on, 'ave a bit.

NICOLA: No, it's all right.

WENDY: Have a little bit, cheer yourself up.

ANDY: She's all right – don't force her.

NATALIE: Here y'are, Nic. (*She gives* NICOLA *her tea.*)

NICOLA: Thanks.

A few minutes later, WENDY *is sitting between the girls on the sofa.*
ANDY *is still in his chair. They all sip their tea.*

WENDY: D'you go up the travel agents?

NATALIE: Yeah. I'm going to New York, Chicago and New
    Orleans.

WENDY: Aren't you goin' Disney?

NATALIE: No, I want to go interesting places.

WENDY: Oh, blimey! Fancy going to the States and not going to
    Disneyland.

ANDY: Why don't you go, Nic?

NICOLA: No . . . it's too big.

WENDY: Well, she can go next year. Get yourself sorted. Save up,
    eh?

NICOLA: 'Ow's the leg?

ANDY: Oh, not too bad. Throbbing a bit. (*Neddy Seagoon voice*)
    There's only one problem! I've got to go to the toilet in a
    minute!
    (WENDY *laughs.*)

WENDY: Hey! Go and get your dad a bucket! (*More laughter.*)
    Hey, look at that spoon! (*She finishes laughing.*)
    (*Pause. The girls exchange glances.*)

Later, WENDY *and* ANDY *are in their bedroom. It is early evening,*
but the curtains are closed. ANDY *is lying on the bed in his pyjamas.*
WENDY *is lifting his plaster-encased leg on to the bed.*

ANDY: Just take the weight, just take the weight . . . That's it,
    that's it.

WENDY: Blimey, it's heavy, innit?

ANDY: Yeah.
    (*The leg is put in position.*)

WENDY: All right?

ANDY: Yeah, put the pillow behind me.

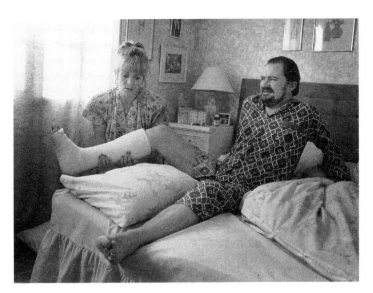

(*She does so.*)
WENDY: There you go.
ANDY: Right.
WENDY: That's it. (*She sits next to him and opens a pill bottle.*) Ha,
I'll tell you what, Andy. Good job you're not a horse.
ANDY: Why?
WENDY: They'd 'ave shot you.
(*They laugh. She gives him a painkiller.*)
Here y'are, then. (*She hands him a glass of water.*) There you
go.
(*He takes the pill. She sighs and puts the lid back on the bottle.
He returns the glass of water, which she puts on the bedside
table.*)

Meanwhile, the girls are sitting together in front of the garden shed.
NICOLA *is smoking a fag.*
NATALIE: It's good you 'ad that chat with Mum, innit? Get things
cleared up. Eh? D'you tell her?
NICOLA: Tell her what?
NATALIE: Everything.
NICOLA: What d'you mean?
NATALIE: You know what I mean.

NICOLA: No.

NATALIE: I'm not deaf.

NICOLA: I never said you was.

NATALIE: I've got the room next to yours, remember? I can hear you.

NICOLA: What, playing my music.

NATALIE: You know what I'm talkin' about. At nights . . . Gettin' sick and everything.

NICOLA: I'm not sick.

NATALIE: Oh, come on.

NICOLA: I'm not.

NATALIE: It's hot, innit.

(*Pause.*)

NICOLA: I can't 'elp it.

NATALIE: I know. I think we should do somethin' about it.

NICOLA: Who's 'we'?

NATALIE: You and me.

NICOLA: Have you told them about it?

NATALIE: No.

NICOLA: Why not?

NATALIE: Oh, I dunno. Suppose I should've . . . don't know why I didn't. Yeah, I do know why. 'Cos I think you should.

NICOLA: I know what I do is disgustin'. I am disgustin'.

NATALIE: Yeah, it is disgustin'. Mind you, I do some pretty disgustin' things meself.

NICOLA: Do you?

NATALIE: Yeah.

NICOLA: What?

NATALIE: Oh, I can't tell you.

NICOLA: What is it?

NATALIE: I put my hands down toilets. And on a good day, I might get bitten by a rat.

(NICOLA *laughs slightly. Pause.*)

D'you want any money?

NICOLA: Yeah.

NATALIE: All right.

NICOLA: Cheers.

NATALIE: No, it's OK.

(*Long pause . . .*

NATALIE *and* NICOLA *sit together quietly at the end of their garden on a pleasant summer's evening.*)